THE OXFAM
MAKE-A-GIFT
BOOK

Compiled by Rachel Edge

CHARLES LETTS
Letts
of London®
FOUNDED 1796

ISBN 1 85238 351 8

Editor: *Pat Pierce*
Designer: *Jo Tapper*
Illustrator: *Sara Sliwinska*
Grid illustrator: *Clive Sutherland*
Photographer: *Julie Fisher*
Stylist: *Simon Lycett*

Prepared for Charles Letts & Company Ltd by
Complete Editions

Acknowledgements
'Ambridge Elderflower Champagne from The Archers' is
from *The Ambridge Book of Country Cooking* by Caroline
Bone, © 1986 William Smethurst, reproduced by permission
of Methuen, London. Photograph page 56 Hereford Times.
Photograph page 91 Rowan Yarns.
   Oxfam photographs: p104 Carol Wills, Oxfam Trading;
p109 Marcus Thompson, Oxfam; p110 Jane Hardy, Oxfam
   The publishers gratefully thank the following: Oxfam
Trading, Rosie Barraud (Cockerel Sweater model), Nicole
Brown (T-shirt model), Robert Day, Marcia Murray, and
Sara Taylor.

First published in 1992
by Charles Letts & Co Ltd,
Letts of London House,
Parkgate Road,
London SW11 4NQ

A CIP catalogue record for this book is available from the
British Library.
ISBN 1 85238 351 8

"Letts" is a registered trademark of Charles Letts & Co
Limited.

Printed and bound in Spain

Title page: Oxfam Rag Rug

CONTENTS

FOREWORD

by Gloria Hunniford and Caron Keating

We are delighted to introduce this special book to mark Oxfam's 50th Anniversary. There are lots of ideas for gifts that all the family can make and, as mother and daughter, we know the pleasure that comes from making, giving and receiving such gifts. But that's not all: every copy sold helps Oxfam continue its valuable work.

Famous and not-so-famous people, and organisations large and small have contributed their different skills to create something to suit everyone. There are gifts to cook, gifts from the garden, gifts to make or paint and gifts to sew or knit.

All the ideas are related to Oxfam's concern for a Fairer World. Some are made by recycling used materials; others make careful use of natural materials, or perhaps it is just that their design reflects the essential idea of a Fairer World for everyone on the planet. So have a go: they are fun to make and even more fun to give.

Giving has been the magic of Oxfam for fifty years: gifts of money that people have worked for and saved; of time to organise collections and events; of goods for sale, and the great gift of work given by thousands of volunteers who run the Oxfam shops.

All this is transformed by Oxfam into gifts of help for those who are suffering, and into gifts of hope for people who have nothing but their own efforts to build a better future.

Thank you for buying the book and helping Oxfam. All royalties will go to the Oxfam Literacy Fund which supports the efforts of young and old in poor communities to read and write. That's a great gift!

Opposite: *Oxfam Anniversary Cake*

GIFTS FROM THE KITCHEN

♥♥♥♥♥♥♥♥♥♥♥♥♥♥♥♥♥♥♥♥♥

OXFAM ANNIVERSARY CAKE

by Rebecca Gowers

When sugar suitable for modelling first reached Europe late in the 12th century it was very rare and valuable, and was used to make festive representations of extreme wealth and power. It was only superceded for this purpose five centuries later when the secrets of Chinese porcelain manufacture were revealed. Though sugar gradually became more and more available after this, and therefore less valuable, it never completely shed its symbolic function, today seen most spectacularly in the wedding cake.

The Oxfam Anniversary Cake has the Oxfam world symbol in the middle, and then, in concentric circles, fish and grain (food), huts (shelter), books (education), buffaloes and fishing skiffs (labour or work), and the sun and the rain (benign weather and fresh water). Each slice gives a share of all these things.

Step-by-step instructions

THE CAKE

The cake illustrated is 37cm (14 1/2 in) in diameter. This cake was made for a special event. The following instructions explain the techniques used in decorating it, which can be adapted to your own designs and a smaller cake. For example, the central design (leaving off the clouds, sun, buffaloes and boats) would fit a 25cm (10in) cake.

Make your cake: sponge, Madeira or fruit cake.

✱ *HINT For a sponge cake: Sugarpaste icing can be laid on directly. For a fruit cake: Put a layer of marzipan on first, having brushed the cake first with apricot jam; brush marzipan with alcohol before covering with sugarpaste.*

DECORATION

INGREDIENTS TO DECORATE A 25CM (10IN) CAKE:
0.75kg (1 1/2 lb) marzipan (optional)
1kg (2lb) purchased sugarpaste, or made to your own recipe
royal icing, purchased or made to your own recipe (for piping)
apricot jam, boiled and strained
alcohol: gin or vodka
icing sugar (to keep your hands dry)
cornflour
icing colouring

MATERIALS:
piping nozzles
cling film (to keep sugarpaste fresh and damp)
card, thin
paintbrush
craft knife
greaseproof paper
scissors
ribbon

GENERAL TECHNIQUES

How to mark out a design:
For a complicated design, such as the one illustrated, it is too difficult to apply the design freehand.
1. Cut a master template out of greaseproof paper the same size as the cake.
2. Draw or measure out your design on the greaseproof paper.
3. With a pin make a series of guide holes at critical points in the design.
4. Lay the master template on the cake and, using a pin, mark through the guide holes on to the icing.
5. For complicated shapes it is advisable to prick around the complete outline.

✱ *HINT For a simpler version, space out the dry decorations on the surface of the icing until you are happy with the arrangement.*

How to colour icing:

Icing can be pre-coloured before decorations are formed OR decorations can be painted when dry OR a combination of both.

Colouring before use: Add gel, liquid or powder to the icing; gel is probably the easiest to use.

Colouring after decorations are made: Gel or liquid can be painted on neat. The effects of this are harsh and, in time, the colours may start to stain adjacent icing

A better method, which allows for both delicate and rich colouring, is to make a little sugarpaste very liquid with egg white, and then add gel, liquid or powder to it. When painted on it forms a glaze.

How to make decorations as runouts:

l. Mix icing to piping consistency.
2. Pipe round the outline of the shape. (See below for Piping.)
3. Add a little egg white to the remains of the icing until it is just liquid enough to paint with.
4. Fill up the shape to the height of the piped outline with icing using a fine paintbrush.

● *NOTES*
1. Making good runouts requires a little experience.
2. If you are worried about piping directly on to the cake, you can pipe runouts on waxed paper. Once dry, peel the paper off the runouts and stick them on to the cake.

3. On the cake illustrated, all runouts were piped directly onto the cake.

How to cut decorations from sugarpaste using templates:

1. Trace the templates onto greaseproof paper.
2. Transfer the shapes to thin card and cut shapes out of the card.
3. Roll out the sugarpaste thinly.
4. Use the templates and a craft knife (scalpel) to cut out shapes of decorations.
5. Leave to dry on greaseproof paper; dust with a bit of cornflour, if necessary.

How to pipe:

To pipe a line: Touch icing to cake and then pull gently away, keeping nozzle just above surface and letting string of icing fall according to your design. To finish line, simply touch the nozzle back down again.

To pipe a dot: Squeeze out a little icing directly onto cake, pull sharply away.

DECORATING THE CAKE:

● *NOTE* *See cake illustrated for colour reference.*

1. Plan the design for your cake using the shapes given in the templates. Mark out the design on your cake. For example, mark the eye and base of the tail for each fish and the complete outline of each buffalo. The stalks of grain can be applied freehand.

The maker
As a cake decorator I am self-taught. I started by making cakes for family celebrations, then graduated to professional work. My designs usually veer towards either the safe, with sugar flowers, sugar insects and shells, piped patterns and messages of goodwill on them, or the dangerous, where the cakes sway around on double tiers three feet above the table, covered in webs of sugar and arrays of candles or fireworks. I make cakes only occasionally, to commission. Otherwise, in the last few months I have had jobs cleaning and mending chandeliers, working as a roof tiler, and doing maid's work in Brompton Square.

2. *Globe, fish, hut base, buffalo body, boat base, sun, cloud:* make as runouts directly on the cake.

✳ *HINT These decorations can also be made as cut-outs and stuck onto the cake once dry. To make the globe as a cut-out: roll out a circle of green sugarpaste. Cut along the Equator, Tropics and lines of longitude. Pull the sections apart and leave to dry before transferring them to the cake.*

3. *Book pages and boat sails:* cut from sugarpaste. Both are left to dry over a small screw of paper to give a billowing-out effect. Once dry, stick on to the cake.

4. Pipe the following decorations onto the cake using royal icing and a plain piping nozzle (see cake illustrated for colour reference): chimneys, hut roofs, drops of rain, stalks of grain, horns, tails and feet of buffaloes, tails and fins of fish and letters on books. For example, the hut roof is a series of lines piped to resemble straw. A stalk of grain is a combination of lines and dots.

5. *Colour your decorations:* On the cake illustrated most of the decorations have been painted. This allows you to modify the colour of the decorations and to give each a slight sheen. For example, the fish were made from pale green icing and then painted with a series of glazes. Some of the bright red speckles were painted on neat and then muted with a thin wash of blue glaze over the top. The huts and buffaloes were made in one colour of icing and then painted with glazes to make each decoration look different.

Use your imagination to colour your decorations using the techniques described earlier.

For a finishing touch, tie a ribbon round the Anniversary Cake.

This cake is not expensive to make, and there is an endless variety to the designs, both simple and complicated, which can be derived from the techniques above to make gift cakes. Inexperienced cake decorators will probably take a long time over their work without entirely meaning to. Experienced cake decorators will probably take a long time over their work on purpose.

You can become really good at icing if you are patient and have calm hands, but you can become pretty good pretty fast without a great deal of practice. The Oxfam Anniversary Cake took two days to make.

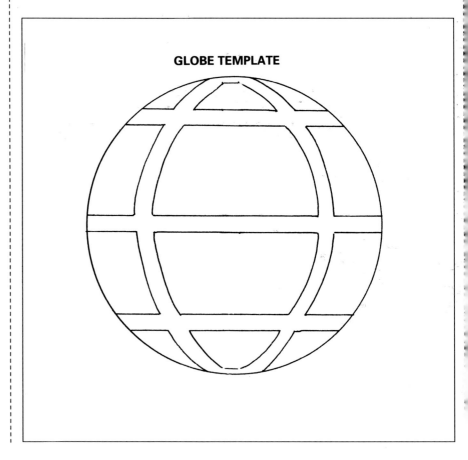

GLOBE TEMPLATE

TEMPLATES

VEGAN TREATS FROM INVERDENE

by Julie Campbell

This package of treats from Inverdene in the Scottish Highlands consists of making Tofu, Leek and Mushroom Tofu Flan, Hazelnut and Lentil Pâté and Apricot Ice Cream.

LEEK AND MUSHROOM TOFU FLAN

This is a gift to be made in two stages: the first is the making of the versatile food known as tofu; the second, using it to make a leek and mushroom tofu flan.

Tofu is made from soya beans, which are protein rich and highly productive agriculturally. Tofu is a healthy cholesterol-free food with no additives; nothing goes to waste. For example, the solid remains of the soya beans, called okara, make great veggie-burgers when mixed with lightly fried chopped vegetables and seasoned; it can also be dried and used as a crumble topping.

There is even more to this remarkable food. The soya whey contains natural sugars, so can be used as the liquid in bread-making to give a lighter texture; added to soups as a stock; and – because of its natural grease-cutting properties – added to the washing!

If you are really enthusiastic, and live in the right climate, such as the south of England, you can grow some varieties of soya bean yourself. As a legume, they also enrich the soil with nitrogen, thus saving on the use of petroleum-based fertilisers.

This recipe reflects Oxfam's 'It's Time for a Fairer World' theme in the following way: a vegan diet contributes to a better use of the land available for growing food. Animal farming is an extravagant and ecologically unsound use of our resources.

Many of the world's food problems could be alleviated if land devoted to animal rearing was turned over to plant-food cultivation. As tofu is one of the most nutritious, versatile and delicious of plant foods, it seems like the best example to include.

Step-by-step instructions

The flan can be made with commercial tofu, which is much easier. It is available in both fresh and powdered form. If you have the time, here's how to make the whole thing. Remember that each 450g (1lb) dry weight of beans should make 900g (2lb) of tofu.

MAKE YOUR OWN TOFU

MATERIALS:
liquidiser
colander
sieve
nylon OR *similar strong material, one piece*
muslin, 1 piece
tofu pressing box OR *large margarine tub with holes poked through base*
large pan

INGREDIENTS:
450g (1lb) soya beans soaked overnight but not cooked
2tbsp nigari (OR 8tbsp lemon juice OR 8tbsp cider vinegar) dissolved in 425ml (³/4pt) cold water. (Nigari is available from good health food shops.)
lots of boiling water

METHOD
1. Put 500ml (2 cups) of soaked soya beans into the liquidiser. Top up to 1 litre (1 1/2pt) boiling water.

Opposite: *Apricot Ice Cream, Hazelnut Pâté and Leek and Mushroom Flan*

(The quantities are not critical.) Liquidise for 2 – 3 minutes.

2. Balance the colander over a pan, line the colander with the nylon and pour in the mixture. Gather up the edges of the material and squeeze as much of the liquid through as possible, either by hand using rubber gloves, or by using a potato masher to push down against the colander.

● *NOTE The resulting liquid is soya milk from which the tofu is made, so it is important to squeeze out as much as possible.*

3. Open material out and stir in another $1/4 - 1/3$ litre ($1/2 - 3/4$ pt) of boiling water. Then squeeze through again.
4. Pour the soya milk into the large pan and keep on a low heat. Put aside the solid remains (okara) for other uses described in the introduction.
5. Repeat the squeezing process until all the soya beans are used up and all the soya milk is in the large pan.
6. Bring the soya milk to the boil, stirring all the time; then simmer for 5 minutes. Remove from the heat.
7. Very slowly pour half the nigari solution over the back of a wooden spoon so that it 'falls like rain' over the surface of the soya milk.
8. Leave for 2 minutes, then repeat with the rest of the nigari. Very gently stir the top inch of the

liquid, then leave to stand for 2 more minutes.

9. Next, put the wooden spoon right to the bottom of the pan and even more gently move it through the mixture until all the soya milk has coagulated into curds and whey.

● *NOTE It is very important not to rush this part and to be very gentle or the 'jelly-like' lumps of curds formed will break up giving a granular texture resulting in an inferior tofu.*

10. Line the tofu pressing box with muslin, leaving enough spare material to cover the top once filled.
11. Press the sieve down into the pan, so that some of the whey can be ladled off with a cup, whilst leaving the tofu undisturbed.
12. Pour the whey through the tofu box to catch any small bits of tofu.
13. Remove the sieve, and gently transfer the tofu into the box using a tea-strainer or a spaghetti spoon.

When completed, cover with muslin and put on a lid of a slightly smaller size than the box. Place a weight on top, for example, a couple of litre cartons of orange juice, and leave to press for 15 minutes.

Transfer the pressed tofu into a suitable container, cover with water and store in the fridge. To keep it fresh, change the water every day, and it will last for about 10 days.

LEEK AND MUSHROOM FLAN

This is a favourite. Summer or winter, it never loses its appeal.

PASTRY BASE:
225g (8oz) wholemeal flour
110g (4oz) hard vegetable fat
approx. 4 tbsp cold water, to mix
Optional: 1 tbsp soya oil (to give more manageable dough)
Optional: 1 tsp bicarbonate of soda
FILLING:
175g (6oz) leeks, washed and chopped
225g (8oz) mushrooms, washed and chopped
a little vegetable oil
TOPPING:
225g (8oz) firm tofu
275ml (1/2pt) unsweetened soya milk
2 tbsp soy sauce
1 tbsp tahani (sesame seed spread)
pumpkin, sesame or sunflower seeds

❋ *HINT Use smoked tofu to give the recipe a more savoury flavour.*

METHOD
Pastry: Place the flour (and bicarbonate of soda) in a bowl, rub in the fat with the oil (if used) until the mixture resembles breadcrumbs. Add enough cold water to mix a soft dough. Roll out and line a 25cm (10in) flan case. Bake blind for 15 minutes at 180C (350F, Gas mark 4).
Filling and topping: Lightly fry the leeks and mushrooms in a little oil for about 5 minutes until just tender; then spread evenly over

The maker
I run Inverdene Vegan Guest House in the Scottish Highlands along with my husband, Stephen. My interest in cooking grew after I became first vegetarian and then vegan. I find this type of food tasty and exciting. I enjoy experimenting with different foods, making up recipes, and - most of all - we both enjoy eating them along with our guests.

We grow most of our own vegetables and try to run the guest house along compassionate and environmentally friendly lines.

the cooked case. Put the rest of the ingredients, bar the seeds, in a blender and whizz until smooth. Pour over leeks and mushrooms. Sprinkle with the seeds. Bake at temperature above for 30 40 minutes or until golden brown. Serve with steamed potatoes and crisp green salad.

This recipe is easy to make and only takes a couple of hours. Use the same recipe to make mini-tarts.

HAZELNUT AND LENTIL PATE

Why buy tiny and expensive tubs of pâté, when it is so easy to make your own? Here is a tasty one to start you off, for your lunchbox or as a starter for a meal.

INGREDIENTS:
110g (4oz) red lentils
110g (4oz) hazelnuts, finely chopped
1 large onion, chopped
1 clove garlic, crushed
2 tsp yeast extract
1 tsp mixed herbs
1 tbsp vegetable oil

METHOD
Fry the onions in oil for 5 minutes before adding the garlic, lentils and herbs. Stir well and add enough water to just cover the ingredients. Bring to the boil and simmer for 20 minutes, adding a little more water if needed.

Remove from the heat. Add the yeast extract and hazelnuts and blend well.

Put into individual dishes and chill before serving. Garnish with a sprig of fresh herbs or a twist of cucumber and serve with a salad and oatcakes or toast.

This pâté is quick and easy to make. It costs very little, and can be made in quantity in advance for a party or a special occasion. Try your own variations and garnishes

APRICOT ICE CREAM

Here is another recipe based on soya.

The commercial vegan ice creams may taste too sweet for you, or simply be unavailable. Julie uses an ice-cream maker, but this ice cream can be made very well without one.

INGREDIENTS:
175g (6oz) dried unsulphured (if available) apricots
600ml (1pt) unsweetened soya milk
1 tbsp orange juice
1 tsp grated orange rind

METHOD
1. Soak apricots in half the soya milk for three hours.
2. Cook for 10 to 15 minutes until softened. Cool slightly.
3. Whizz up in a blender with the remaining soya milk, adding it a little at a time to give a smooth texture.
4. Stir in 1 tbsp orange juice and 1 tsp grated rind.
5. Put into an ice-cream maker or a plastic tub in the freezer.
6. Beat it several times as it is freezing.
7. Stand at room temperature to soften slightly before serving, which also helps release the flavour.

It is a very unusual occurence if this ice cream is not eaten all in one go.

FRUIT CAKE

from the Vegan Society

This delicious fruit cake, designed by Janet Hunt for the Vegan Society, is completely vegan, which means that it contains no animal ingredients whatsoever. It does not exploit animals and uses less of the earth's resources, so it is also kinder to the environment.

The Maker
Janet Hunt is a freelance cookery writer living in Avon, who has written a numer of cookery books including *The Caring Cook* and *The Diet Free Cook Book*. She has written a regular cookery column for the Vegan Society's quarterly magazine, *The Vegan*, for several years.

The Contributor
Founded in 1944, the Vegan Society promotes ways of living which seek, as far as is possible and practical, to dispense with all animal products, whether for food, clothing or other purposes. It publishes leaflets, books and a magazine and has a network of contacts throughout the country.

In Oxfam's Anniversary Year with it's theme 'It's Time for a Fairer World', the Vegan Society continues to support the essential message of ecology - that everthing is interconnected. This obliges each of us to take responsibility for the world around us. Vegans have chosen to dispense with animal produce, and thus do something practical to reduce the damage our species is causing to the environment, our fellow animals and ourselves.

THE **Vegan** SOCIETY

Step-by-step instructions

INGREDIENTS:
225g (8oz) vegan margarine
575ml (1pt) cold water
225g (8oz) sugar
2 tsp syrup, golden
680g (1 1/2 lb) mixed dried fruit (eg. raisins, currants, sultanas, chopped dates, apricots)
1 tsp cinnamon
1 tsp ginger
1 tsp allspice
1/2 tsp nutmeg
2 tsp vanilla essence
2 tsp bicarbonate of soda
rind and juice of one lemon
395g (14oz) wholemeal flour
50g (2 oz) soya flour
50g (2oz) chopped almonds
50g (2oz) chopped walnuts
1 tbsp brandy or liqueur (optional)

METHOD
1. Put the margarine, water, sugar, syrup, fruit and spices into a large saucepan.
2. Melt margarine and then boil for 10 minutes. Leave to cool for 15 minutes.
3. Mix into the remaining ingredients, making sure the mixture is thoroughly blended.
4. Lightly grease a 20-23cm (8-9in) cake tin and pour in the mixture. Level the surface.
5. Bake at 150C (325F, Gas mark 2) for 2 hours, or until a fine needle inserted in the centre comes out clean.

The Vegan Society Fruit Cake is easy enough for a beginner to make, takes about three hours in all, and is not too expensive. It is delicious.

Opposite: *Chewy Fruit Fingers, Chocolate Easter Cake, Fruit Cake.*

ONE HEALTHY SWEET – AND A NAUGHTY ONE

from Blue Peter

Here are two recipes from the Blue Peter kitchens. Both of these projects have been featured on Blue Peter. There is one 'healthy' recipe - for Chewy Fruit Fingers – and a recipe for an unashamedly luxurious chocolate cake. Our excuse for including this one is that you can buy cocoa powder in your local Oxfam shop!

CHEWY FRUIT FINGERS

INGREDIENTS:
75g (3oz) self-raising flour
75g (3oz) rolled oats
125g (4oz) firm margarine
75g (3oz) demerara sugar
125g (4oz) dried apricots
50g (2oz) dates

METHOD
1. Lightly grease a shallow tin 18cm x 18cm (7in x 7in).
2. Put the flour, oats and fat into a mixing bowl.
3. Chop fat into dry ingredients with knife; mix very lightly with fingers until the ingredients are well-mixed and crumbly.
4. Stir in the sugar.
5. Spread half the mixture over the base of the prepared tin.
6. Chop apricots and dates.
7. Mix the chopped fruit and spread over oat mixture.
8. Sprinkle remaining oat mixture over fruit and press down firmly.
9. Bake at 180C (350F, gas mark 4) for about 30 minutes or until golden brown.
10. Cool in tin. Then cut into bars.

Chewy Fruit Fingers are cheap, quick and easy. And they taste good.

CHOCOLATE EASTER CAKE

INGREDIENTS:
275g (10oz) self-raising flour
225g (8oz) caster sugar
1 1/2 tsp baking powder
*200g (7oz) jar of mayonnaise (*NOT *salad cream)*
4 tbsp cocoa
225ml (8fl oz) boiling water
1 tsp vanilla essence

METHOD
1. Line a 18cm (7in) cake tin with grease-proof paper, greasing the tin side of the paper; otherwise it will stick to the tin.
2. Turn on oven to pre-heat to 180C (350 F, gas mark 4).

FLOUR MIXTURE:
1. Measure self-raising flour into a large mixing-bowl. Add caster sugar and baking powder.
2. Give the whole mixture a quick stir and then add the mayonnaise.

3. Beat the mayonnaise well into the flour, sugar and baking powder. It is very important to beat the mayonnaise thoroughly into the ingredients. Make sure that this flour mixture is well blended - it should look like large breadcrumbs. Put to one side while you make the chocolate mixture.

CHOCOLATE MIXTURE:
Dissolve the cocoa in the boiling water. Stir this gently until it's smooth and there are no lumps of cocoa.
THEN:
1. Add the chocolate mixture to the flour mixture.
2. Give the whole mixture a quick stir and then add the vanilla essence. Stir everything thoroughly until all the ingredients are blended, but this time DON'T beat the mixture because that will spoil it. Just keep stirring it gently until all the lumps are gone.
3. Pour mixture into prepared tin. Place in middle of pre-heated oven. Cook for about one hour,

until a fine skewer inserted in the centre comes out clean.

4. Cool in tin before turning out, otherwise it will crumble. The cake is now ready for icing.

ICING

INGREDIENTS:

2 level tsp instant coffee
2 level tbsp cocoa
2 tbsp hot water
75g (3oz) soft margarine
225g (8oz) icing sugar

METHOD

1. Dissolve instant coffee and cocoa in hot water. Add margarine and icing sugar.

2. Beat the mixture thoroughly ensuring that no lumps are left and then spread the mixture over the top and sides of the cake.

✱ *HINT For a really professional job: Add little sugar eggs, and maybe a tiny fluffy chicken.*

The Blue Peter Chocolate Easter Cake may take 1 1/2 to 2 hours to make, and may cost a little bit more than an ordinary cake - but anyone can make it, and the result is worth it

AMBRIDGE ELDERFLOWER CHAMPAGNE

from The Archers

You will only need four of heads of elderflower to make this sparkling, thirst-quenching summer drink. Summer is not truly come (so they say) until the elder is in flower, and it ends only when the elderberries are ripe. The heavily-scented blossoms, creamy among the dark leaves, appear in May or early June, depending on where you live.

The Contributor
Our request for entries to *The Oxfam Make-a-Gift Book* was picked up by the Borchester Oxfam Shop. They were lucky to be given a recipe that was always one of Pru Forrest's favourites. She got it from Mary Pound who used to live at Ambridge Farm with her husband, Ken.

Step-by-step instructions

INGREDIENTS:

four large heads elderflower (picked when they are just out)
1 lemon
675g (1 1/2 lb) white sugar
2 tbsp white wine vinegar
4 1/2 litres (l gallon) cold water

METHOD

1. Pick the heads when the blossom has newly opened. Take off the green stems, if there are any, and put the heads into a bowl.

● *NOTE For best flavour, it is important that the blossoms be newly opened.*

2. Sprinkle with juice from the lemon.

3. Grate the rind, and add together with vinegar and sugar.

4. Add the cold water. Leave for 24 hours.

5. Strain into clean bottles. Cork firmly. Lay the bottles on their sides.

Within two weeks the 'champagne' should be sparkling and ready to drink.

● *NOTE Unopened bottles will keep for up to 3 months.*

The Ambridge Elderflower Champagne is easy to make and inexpensive. You will never forget your sparkling champagne.

GOOSEBERRY CHUTNEY

by Pat Clarke

This scrumptious chutney is easy to make and will store for months. As a food, it is wholesome and simple. Various fruits and vegetables, which can be homegrown, are mixed together with ginger or spices from other lands, to give an exotic taste to meals, especially during winter months. It may perhaps be a reminder of our friends in need.

The recipe for this gooseberry chutney was given to me around 40 years ago and is a family favourite. The chutney is made with love and care, and the jars can be decorated with attractive paper. Trim the lid with coloured ribbons, a posy of dried flowers or beads, perhaps letting them tumble down the sides of the jar. Let your imagination run riot.

Step-by-step instructions

INGREDIENTS:
*1350g (3lb) gooseberries, cut in half,
  OR green tomatoes OR hard plums,
  for example
450g (1lb) onions, chopped coarsely
600ml (1pt) malt vinegar
900g (2lb) soft dark brown sugar
25g (1oz) ground ginger
25g (1oz) salt
225g (8oz) sultanas
pinch freshly ground black pepper*

METHOD
1. Place the gooseberries and onions in a large stainless steel saucepan or preserving pan. Add vinegar, sugar, ginger, sultanas, salt and pepper.

✳ *HINT Increase the ginger for a 'hotter' chutney.*

2. Bring to the boil and simmer gently, stirring frequently until the chutney is dark brown and the liquid reduced. This will take up to one hour.
3. Taste to adjust salt, if necessary.
4. Put chutney into clean, warm jars and immediately cover with waxed discs and airtight lids. It is best to keep chutney for at least one month before eating.

The maker
I am an amateur cook with 40 years experience cooking for family and friends, and am an enthusiastic supporter of Oxfam. I can think of nothing more enjoyable than sitting round the table with friends to enjoy a home-cooked meal, a bottle of wine (or two) and good conversation – trying to 'put the world to rights'.

Now that I am retired I have more time for my garden and greenhouse, drying and arranging flowers, and my cat Myffanwy (called Muffin).

What more could one ask for from life - good friends, love and good food? So many people are without all these things, and that's something we should strive harder to put right.

Gooseberry Chutney is very easy to make, costs very little, takes about 1 1/2 hours in all to make, and tastes delicious.

Opposite: *Hedgerow Jelly, Ambridge Elderflower Champagne and Gooseberry Chutney*

HEDGEROW JELLY

by Aileen Gault for FWINI

The fruits of the hedgerow combine to make this delicious jelly. The colours and flavours of the fruits are instantly evocative of the natural goodness available to each and every one of us.

The Maker and Contributor
Mrs Aileen Gault, the maker of this fine jelly, has been a member of the Women's Institute for many years. She attends Ballykelly WI on the outskirts of Limavady, County Londonderry. Aileen is a keen craftswoman and serves on the Executive and Homecraft Committees of the Federation of Women's Institutes of Northern Ireland (FWINI).
The FWINI has for decades played an important role in rural life through its educational and social centres for countrywomen.

Step-by-step instructions

INGREDIENTS:
1kg (2lb) crab or windfall apples
1kg (2lb) blackberries
1kg (2lb) sloes, elderberries, hips and haws OR any selection of berries from hedgerow
400g (1lb) sugar per 475ml (16 fl oz) liquid (See method.)

METHOD
1. Wash and quarter apples, clean blackberries and sloes, remove stems from elderberries, top and tail hips and clean haws; give all a final wash.
2. Put into preserving pan, cover with water and cook slowly until soft (20-30 minutes).
3. Strain through muslin jelly bag overnight, but remember not to squeeze bag.
4. Measure liquid and add sugar accordingly – 400g (1lb) sugar to each 475ml (16 fl oz) of liquid. Stir until sugar is dissolved.
5. Boil rapidly for about 30 minutes until set. Test on a cold plate.
6. Pot in clean warm jars and seal immediately.

✳ *HINT For additional flavours: Add various spices, such as root ginger, cloves or cinammon. Tie spices in a muslin bag, and add to the liquid with the sugar. Remove bag before potting.*

Hedgerow Jelly has a lovely flavour and colour - almost too good to eat. It is easy to make, and costs very little.

Opposite: Herb Teas and Nature's Picture

GIFTS FROM THE GARDEN

♥♥♥♥♥♥♥♥♥♥♥♥♥♥♥♥♥♥♥♥♥♥♥♥♥

A TASTE OF HERB TEAS

from The Herb Society

We are lucky because there are herbal teas for every occasion. The Anniversary Blend, specially named for Oxfam's 50th Anniversary, is a most refreshing drink to start the day. Tea of Happiness, based on a recipe by the famous French herbalist Maurice Mességué, lifts the spirits. Encourage sweet dreams and restful sleep with Good-Night Tea. All are caffeine-free and can be used safely, although excessive quantities should be avoided during pregnancy.

Some General Information about Herbs

Gathering herbs:
Most herbs are gathered just before flowering. Pick on a dry day or after the dew has cleared, so the plants dry quickly to retain their scent and flavour.

✻ *HINT Consult any good herb book (such as* Growing Herbs *by Eric Groves, published by the Society) for detailed guidelines.*

Drying herbs:
To dry herbs, hang them in small bunches away from direct sunlight, but where there is a good circulation of air, or spread them on narrow trays and leave in an airing cupboard with the door ajar.

Dry thoroughly: if bagged or bottled while still slightly damp they will quickly go mouldy. The leaves should be brittle, but not so dry that they turn to powder when touched.

Once dried, the various herbs can be blended thoroughly and packed in cellophane or plastic bags or, even better, bottled in air-tight containers, preferably made of glass or china. Remember to label them. For gifts, fill small glass jars, make pretty labels and decorate the containers.

✻ *HINT If bottled in clear glass, keep out of the sunlight. Never use metal containers.*

● *NOTE Excessive quantities of many herbs should be avoided during pregnancy. If in doubt, consult a qualified herbalist.*

For all recipes:
Examples of 1 part
To make a larger amount,
  1 part = 100g (4oz)
To make a smaller amount,
  1 part = 1tbsp, rounded

ANNIVERSARY BLEND

INGREDIENTS:
1 part Chamomile flowers
  (Chamomilla recutita)
1 part Raspberry leaf (Rubus idaeus)
1 part Marigold petals (Calendula
  officinalis)
1 part Cornflower flowers
  (Centaurea cyanus)
1 part Peppermint herb (Mentha X
  piperita)
2 parts Hibiscus flowers
  (Abelmoschus moscheutos)
2 parts Strawberry leaf (Fragaria
  vesca)

METHOD
Mix the dried herbs and pack in cellophane bags, or bottle.
To use: infuse 1-2 tsp of the tea to 250ml (1 cup) of water which is slightly off the boil, for 5 minutes. Strain and drink.

Our Anniversary Blend is easy to make and inexpensive. This tea makes every day an occasion.

TEA OF HAPPINESS

INGREDIENTS:
1 part Lavender flowers (Lavandula officinalis)
1 part Chamomile flowers (Chamomilla recutita)
2 parts Lime blossom (Tilia europaea)
2 parts Betony (Stachys betonica) OR *Vervain herb (Verbena officinalis)*
1 part Peppermint herb (Mentha X piperita)

METHOD
Mix the dried herbs and pack in cellophane bags, or bottle.
To use: infuse 1 – 2 tsp of the tea to 250ml (1 cup) of water which is slightly off the boil, for 5 minutes. Strain and drink.

GOOD-NIGHT TEA

INGREDIENTS:
3 parts Passionflower herb (Passiflora incarnata)
1 part Chamomile flowers (Chamomilla recutita)
2 parts Lime blossom (Tilia europaea)
1 part Lavender flowers (Lavandula officinalis)
1 part Peppermint herb (Mentha X piperita)

METHOD
Mix the dried herbs and pack in cellophane bags, or bottle.
To use: infuse 1 – 2 tsp of the tea to 250ml (1 cup) of water which is slightly off the boil, for 5 minutes. Strain and drink.

These teas are easy to make, cost almost nothing, and open the door to the world of herbs.

The Contributor
The Herb Society brings together all those who have an interest in herbs. Its international membership includes professional growers, medical herbalists, beauticians and cooks, as well as those who are only beginning to discover the fascination of herbs.
The Society publishes *Herbs*, the UK's only specialist publication devoted to all aspects of herbs.
Based in London, the Society was founded in 1927 and has been a registered educational charity since 1976.

Properties of herbs used in the teas:
Betony – tonic nervine, used for headaches
Chamomile flowers – digestive tonic, sedative, antispasmodic
Cornflower flowers – tonic, stimulant, digestive remedy
Hibiscus flowers – nervine (soothes the nerves), digestive remedy
Lavender flowers – sedating nervine, carminative, used for nervous complaints and headaches
Lime blossom – diaphoretic, hypotensive remedy (for abnormally low blood pressure)
Marigold petals – astringent and digestive stimulant.
Passionflower herb – Sedating nervine, good for insomnia.
Peppermint leaves – stimulating, warming, diaphoretic, carminative, antispasmodic
Raspberry leaves – astringent, stimulant, digestive remedy. NOTE This is a uterine stimulant; use with caution in pregnancy.
Strawberry leaves – mild laxative, diuretic and astringent.

NATURE'S PICTURE

by Hilda Carter for NAFAS

Here grasses and seeds combine beautifully in a good, simple design to make a picture which is set off by the recessed frame. The three ears of corn are one of Oxfam's designs for its 50th Anniversary. Pressed flowers can also be used to make very attractive pictures, which when framed make appealing gifts.

Step-by-step instructions

Decide on the size of picture you want, and choose your frame before you begin. Collect your seeds and grasses, so you have a variety to select from.

MATERIALS:
seeds and grasses
frame, glass and hardboard backing
tracing paper
material on which to work the design
*   (something like polyester cotton,*
*   thin enough so the design can be*
*   seen through it for tracing)*
vilene
PVA glue
fablon

METHOD
1. Trace the design onto tracing paper.
2. Remove glass and hardboard backing from frame.
3. Place the hardboard backing on the piece of material.
4. Draw the shape of the hardboard backing onto the material and cut out.
5. Draw the same shape onto the vilene and cut out.

6. Very lightly trace the design onto the material; then iron the vilene onto the back of the design to prevent fraying of edges.
7. Collect all the seeds and grasses and keep in separate containers, which will be easy to work from.

✳ *HINT Work from the top of the design to the bottom.*

8. Put a little glue on a saucer or lid; using the point of a needle or cocktail stick, lift a tiny blob and lay it on the design. Lift a seed or grass with tweezers; lay it on the glue blob. Use a minimal amount of glue. Don't mark the fabric.
9. Lay the completed design on the hardboard backing. Clean the glass and lay it on the design. Place the frame in position, then carefully turn the whole thing over. The backing should be flush with the frame and held in by staples or panel pins. If it is not flush, cut another cardboard shape to pad it out.
11. Cover hardboard backing with baize peel-off fablon or chromolux for a professional finish, and to

keep dust and moisture out. Add hanging ring or rings.

This picture, or one similar, can be made with care quite easily. Once you have your design, it takes about 2-3 hours to do.

The Maker and Contributor
Hilda Carter is Area Secretary of the National Association of Flower Arrangement Societies of Great Britain (NAFAS). She has arranged flowers in Westminster Abbey, Salisbury Cathedral and Christ Church Cathedral, Oxford. In 1992 she represented NAFAS by staging an exhibit in Philadelphia, USA. NAFAS promotes the skill and pleasure of floral art through education and demonstration.

YOUR ANNIVERSARY SEEDLINGS

from the Henry Doubleday Research Association

This gift will enable you to save your own flower, fruit and vegetable seeds and pass them on to a friend or relative as a living plant.
Saving your own seeds means that you can enjoy the benefits of free seed, as well as perpetuating varieties that are well-suited to your climate and conditions. As gifts, plant varieties are spread to a larger audience and increase plant diversity.
In many developing countries, valuable traditional varieties of crops have been lost when replaced by high-yielding, imported strains. Having a diversity of plant material throughout the world is important because it enables us to use the natural variability within plant species to cope with the changing patterns in pests, diseases and climate.

Step-by-step instructions

PAPER POT
Paper pots are cheap, bio-degradeable and can be planted out with the plants to avoid disturbing roots. They are simple to make.

MATERIALS:
cardboard tube, for example, inner from a toilet roll
newspaper

METHOD
1. Tear/cut strip to height of pot required, plus 3 – 5cm (1 – 2in) for base.
2. Roll paper around tube, leaving 3 – 5cm (1 – 2in) overhanging end of tube.
3. Twist round overhanging paper and tuck in snugly to make flat base.
4. The finished pot.

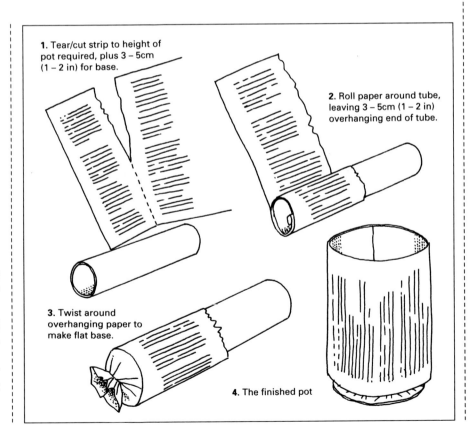

1. Tear/cut strip to height of pot required, plus 3 – 5cm (1 – 2 in) for base.

2. Roll paper around tube, leaving 3 – 5cm (1 – 2 in) overhanging end of tube.

3. Twist around overhanging paper to make flat base.

4. The finished pot

The Contributor

The Henry Doubleday Research Association (HDRA), Europe's largest organic organisation, is situated at the National Centre for Organic Gardening (NCOG).

It promotes and researches environmentally safe gardening and commercial horticultural techniques at its headquarters at Ryton Gardens near Coventry, where 10 acres of demonstration gardens are open to the public.

HDRA gives advice on all aspects of organic gardening and carries out scientific research into improved sustainable growing techniques. The overseas section helps developing countries with practical advice to farmers about the most suitable trees to grow in drought-stricken conditions.

Organic principles apply the world over, and are particularly appropriate for people living in developing countries, who are unable to afford expensive man-made chemicals. Organic growing represents the only truly sustainable way of cultivating land.

In 1975 the HDRA Seed Library was established in order to maintain in cultivation varieties of vegetables whose seed can no longer be sold legally in the UK, as a result of the plant varieties legislation. Members of HDRA can become involved in helping to maintain stock of these rare varieties.

COLLECTING YOUR SEED

Saving your own seed is fun, and one of the easiest is tomato. Growing tomatoes for seed is no different from growing them for eating. To produce the best quality seed, just aim to grow them as well as you can. Avoid growing hybrid varieties, as their offspring or seed will not breed true to their parents. If you have no plants, you can always use seed from tomatoes you have bought at the supermarket. (NOTE: Some tomato varieties sold by supermarkets come from hybrid parent plants.)

METHOD

1. Let the fruit get fully ripe, even a bit over-ripe, before you gather it for seed. Then, cut it in half as if you were going to make tomato slices. Scoop the seeds and surrounding gelatinous pulp from each section into a container (for example, a plastic yoghurt pot). Add some water, if there is not much juice, to prevent it drying out.
2. Label the container and set it in a warm place for several days, but no longer than 4 days or the seed may begin to sprout. A foul-smelling mould will begin to grow over the top! This fungus performs several functions; it eats away the gelatinous coat which surrounds each tomato seed, destroys germination inhibitors present in the seed coat and also eliminates some seed-borne diseases.
3. After the seed has become good and mouldy, empty the contents of the container into a strainer. Hold the strainer under a running tap and swish the contents gently with your hand. The pulp will wash through the mesh and the seeds will come clean. After washing, flip the strainer over and knock the seeds onto a paper towel, spread them out and leave to dry before storing.

✱ *HINT If seeds are laid out individually on a tissue, the seed will tend to stick to it. They can be stored still stuck to the tissue, which can then be cut up into individual seeds for easy sowing.*

SOWING YOUR SEED

1. Fill your pot with an organic multi-purpose compost, firm it in gently, sow two seeds to a pot and cover with compost to its own depth. Water your seeds.
2. Then place the pots side by side on a tray (a shallow-bottomed margarine tub is ideal), and cover with a polythene bag.
3. Store them in a warm place until they have started to germinate. Thin to one seedling per pot and remove the polythene.
4. Place your seedlings either in your greenhouse, if you have one, or fill an empty orange box (easily obtained from most grocers or

supermarkets) with soil and stand your pots on top of the soil.

5. Cut the bottom off old clear plastic lemonade bottles and place one over each of your pots, pushing the bottle into the soil so it will not blow away. Don't forget to remove the screw-top, so your plants can breathe.

6. Put the orange box in a sunny position outdoors. The bottles will act as mini-greenhouses for your tender little plants. Tomato seeds germinate after about eight days.

✱ *HINT When your seeds have germinated, give them a warm position with plenty of light.*

Once your plants are up and growing, they are ready to give away.

✱ *HINT Grow oranges and lemons for presents. Eat your orange or lemon, collect the pips, sow straight away. These seeds will need a longer period of warmth for germination, about three weeks.*

Have you ever thought of growing from seed some of our native trees – ash, beech, chestnut, oak, hawthorn and many more? Collect the fallen seeds from the woods; sow them in your pots. Save the environment. Plant a tree.

Tomato seed when grown into a plant is a useful and thoughtful gift. What could be better to give than a living thing which will produce food?

Above: *Paper Pots and Tomato Seedlings*

27

TYRE TUB FOR FLOWERS

from Blue Peter

Every spring we always seem to need more planters than we have. Here is an easy way to have as many colourful tubs as you want. Can you imagine turning an old wheel and tyre into an attractive planter? Well, now we show you how.

The contributor
Blue Peter has, over the years, suggested many clever and easy ways to create new things from old. The ingenious Tyre Tub was a project featured on Blue Peter.

Step- by- step instructions

MATERIALS:
old wheel and tyre, deflated by
*   unscrewing the valve (any kind*
*   except radial tyres)*
bucket
chalk
gloves
very sharp knife
paint, vinyl emulsion

METHOD
1. Place the tyre flat on top of the bucket for support and then chalk out the first cutting line around the inside edge of the tyre.

2. Wearing gloves and using a very sharp knife, cut around the chalk line, leaving about 5cm (2in) of rubber attached to the wheel hub all the way around.

3. Cut 8 'V' shapes.

4. Remove circular piece of tyre.

5. If the tyre has an inner tube, remove it.

6. Turn the tyre inside out - the easiest way is to stand it on something like a small oil drum. It is a job for two strong adults.

7. Then, it can be painted white, terracotta or just left black.

8. Place a few slates in the bottom for drainage, then fill your tub with earth or compost.

✻ *HINT Try terracotta or brick red paint. Put a little sand in it for a textured effect.*

Making a Tyre Tub may cost nothing at all – just a little of your time.

***Opposite:** Tyre Tub*

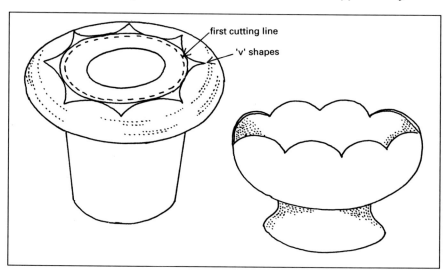

first cutting line

'v' shapes

CERAMIC TILE PLANTERS

from Blue Peter

Blue Peter has come up with another idea for a planter, this time for inside the house. They look great, and are very easy to make. You can make the planter almost any size you like – small for little cactii, or large, for keeping a selection of herbs on the windowsill or for individual plants. It is an idea that makes use of cheap or old ceramic tiles. If you have ever retiled the kitchen or bathroom, you are sure to have some!

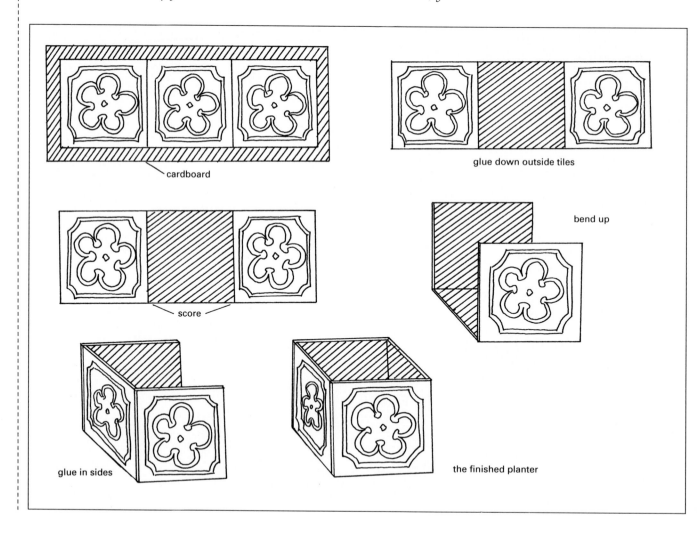

cardboard

glue down outside tiles

score

bend up

glue in sides

the finished planter

Step-by-step instructions

MATERIALS:

4 tiles (from Do-It-Yourself shops or tile shops where there are often ends of lines, or rejects)
cardboard
gloss paint
strong glue
felt
plastic carton or tray

METHOD

1. Take 3 tiles and lay them side by side on the cardboard. Draw round them.

2. Remove the tiles and cut out the cardboard. Paint one side of the cardboard, preferably with gloss paint. (This will become the inside of the planter, where the shine will look good.)

3. Now lay 3 of the tiles on the other side of the cardboard and glue down the 2 outside tiles with a good strong glue; put on lots of glue.

✻ *HINT While you are glueing the 2 outside tiles, leave the centre tile in place to make sure that you put the outside tiles in the right place.*

4. Whilst the glue is drying, take the middle tile and the 4th tile and glue them separately to pieces of cardboard that you have also painted on the other side.

5. Leave all the tiles at least half an hour, so they are well and truly stuck.

The Contributor
Blue Peter, originator of the phrase, 'Here's one I made earlier', has been showing us how to make useful things out of odd bits of inexpensive material since 1963. Here is another winner for *The Oxfam Make-a-Gift Book* from Blue Peter. Ceramic Tile Planters have also been featured on the television show.

6. Return to your first 2 tiles. Score down the sides of the tiles. Bend the tiles up. The middle part of the cardboard is now the base.

7. Put glue round the edge of one of the single tiles and slot it in place between the 2 sides. Get a couple of weights to hold the sides in place while the glue sets, for example, use paint tins.

8. Now glue the other tile in place and once again leave the planter for quite a while to make sure the glue has time to dry.

9. When it is dry, glue a piece of felt to the bottom of the planter to stop it from scratching the furniture.

10. Now find something to put inside the planter to make it waterproof. For a single planter, the lids from cheese cartons could fit perfectly. You can use anything that fits the hole and makes a flower-pot tray (maybe even a proper flower-pot tray).

✻ *HINT For an even quicker result, use a glue gun to fix the tiles together.*

The variety and pattern is endless. You'll never look at tiles the same way again!

'STONE' PLANTER

from The Royal Horticultural Society

This is a gift that will grace your garden for many years to come. The 'Stone' Planter is, unbelievably, made from a discarded sink. The coating you put on the sink gives it a charm and an 'age' which belies its origins. Greenery and flowers tumbling over the 'stone' add character to any garden.

Step-by-step instructions

MATERIALS:
old glazed or domestic sink
sphagnum peat
sharp sand
cement
micafill (sold for insulation purposes at builders merchants)
Unibond (at most ironmongers)
electric drill and masonry bit

● NOTES
1.The Society is taking an active part in examining potential peat alternatives for all aspects of garden usage. It is possible that finer grades of coir may provide a satisfactory alternative to peat in the preparation of simulated stone troughs and the Society will be looking into this aspect of their construction in the near future.
2. Oxfam suggests that you help by trying alternatives to peat.

METHOD

✳ *HINT If the sink is heavy, put it in situ mounted on old bricks or stones, about 15 - 23cm (6 -9in) high, before you begin work on it.*

1. Remove any metal fittings. Wash the sink thoroughly and allow to dry.
2. Use an electric drill and masonry bit to chip away some of the glaze where possible; this will help to achieve better adhesion.
3. Apply a coating of Unibond over about 200cm^2 (2sq ft) of the surface of the glaze. Allow this to become tacky, whilst doing step 4.
4. Mix the cement-based covering mixture, sometimes termed 'hypertufa' (all parts by volume):

NOTE 1 part = 3 litres (5 ^{1}/$_4$ pt)
STANDARD MIX:
1 part sphagnum peat
1 part sharp sand
1 part cement
LIGHTWEIGHT MIX:
1 part peat
^{1}/$_2$ part sharp sand
1 part cement
^{1}/$_2$ part micafill

Avoid making the mixture too wet. A 9-litre (2 gal) bucketful of the complete mixture is APPROXIMATELY sufficient for coating an average-sized sink (60cm [2ft] long, 45cm [18in] wide, 25 - 30cm [10 - 12in] in height), so start with a half bucketful, treating a section at a time.
5. Apply the mixture to the now tacky Unibond. This should extend over the rim and 5 - 7cm (2 - 3in) down the INSIDE, and 7 - 10cm (3 - 4in) UNDER the base, so that on the finished sink no glazed surface is visible. Two or three coatings will give greater durability and resistance to frost damage.
6. To simulate stonework, mark/jab the surface with an old paintbrush or chisel, as the material dries.
7. To give an appearance of age, use a paintbrush to apply neat a coating of milk, manure, water or seaweed liquid feed. This will encourage growth of algae and mosses.

✳ *HINT Treatment is best carried out during cool, but not frosty, weather, as the coating mixture remains workable longer than in warm dry conditions.*

8. Drying usually takes about three weeks. Then plant out sink.

✳ *HINT The peat in the mixture gives the 'stone' colouring; variations in the quantity of peat can give corresponding variations in colour to the finished product.*

● *NOTE Excessive use of peat in the mixture will give a less durable finish.*

The final beauty of the 'Stone' Planter will be a lasting reward for taking the time and care to make it.

Below: 'Stone' Planter

THE ROYAL HORTICULTURAL SOCIETY

The Contributor

The Royal Horticultural Society (RHS) was established in 1804. Its headquarters are at Vincent Square in London, where the finest horticultural library in the world is housed. The Society publishes its journal, *The Garden*, and many other horticultural works.

In 1904 the Society acquired its Garden at Wisley, Surrey, where the Laboratory and the School of Horticulture were set up. The Garden, which occupies 97 hectares (240 acres), includes trials grounds, several model gardens, including fruit and vegetable gardens, large areas of ornamental plantings and woodland gardens, a rock garden, an arboretum and extensive glasshouse range. The garden is open to visitors throughout the year (Members only on Sundays). Since 1988 Wisley has had a unique counterpart in the West Country – Rosemoor, near Great Torrington in Devon.

RHS flower shows have been held since the 1830s, the most famous today being The Chelsea Flower Show.

A HARVEST OF POT POURRI

by Beth Chatto

I make two kinds of pot-pourri, one based on flower-petals, the other using primarily aromatic leaves. Whether you collect plant material from your garden, or from the wild, the choice will be limited to those plants that can be grown in your area, while the surest guide to what is suitable will be your nose. Experimenting with many perfumed flowers and aromatic leaves is necessary. Not all plants retain their perfume when dried; while some, like the unscented scarlet pot geraniums (pelargoniums) or rich blue delphiniums I dry to add bright colour. Anything which keeps its colour well is invaluable to the look of the final product. Do not emulate the virulently dyed and scented curls and chips of wood that are dished up in hotel bathrooms in place of the real thing.

Step-by-step instructions

Pot-pourri using chiefly flower petals

For flower based pot-pourri, I use chiefly the petals from any richly-scented roses.

Throughout the summer collect flower petals, both for perfume and colour effect.

1. Pick them when quite dry (not damp with dew), and spread them to dry in a warm airy place.

I spread mine over the spare beds, on dust sheets. They look like exotic eiderdowns.

2. Whatever scented flowers you use, it is important to pull them well apart to enable them to dry thoroughly and quickly.

✳ *HINT Flowerbuds for decoration should be dried separately; they take longer.*

3. When thoroughly dry, I store them in strong polythene bags, and add little cotton bags of silica gel, before closing them tightly, to wait until more ingredients are available.

These will include lavender (*Lavendula*), pinks (*Dianthus*), and Bergamot (*Monarda*).

The fixative:

Before combining your ingredients, you will need to obtain a fixative, a substance which helps prevent the volatile oils in the plants from evaporating too quickly in the air.

One of the easiest to use and obtain is ground Orris root. This is made from the rhizomes of *Iris dalmatica* or *I. pallida*, both grown in gardens. You can buy Orris root (at the chemists) or make it yourself in late summer.

METHOD FOR ORRIS ROOT FIXATIVE
1. Collect the rhizomes of *Iris dalmatica* or *I. pallida* at the end of summer.

2. Remove the stringy roots, and peel off the skin.

3. Slice them into bits and dry thoroughly, when they can be chopped fine or ground into a powder.

4. Add about 1 tbsp of fixative to 1.5 litres (2 3/4 pt) of petals.

✳ *HINT Another garden plant, Sweet flag (Acorus calamus), can be used in the same way as a fixative. This is not an iris, though it has rhizomes and leaves similar in shape. Both leaves and roots are very sweetly scented, but need moister conditions than the iris, in which to grow.*

● *NOTE Gum benzoin obtained from Styrax benzoin, a tree native to Siam and Sumatra can also be used as a fixative (buy it at the chemists).*

Other ingredients

Orange and lemon peel (with pith removed) can be dried easily on a flat tray in a warm room. When brittle, this can be used in small pieces or pulverized into a powder. It adds a particularly welcome sweet and sharp perfume to the finished pot-pourri.

Finally, you can add spices, either whole or ground. These may include cinnamon, cardamon, coriander, fennel and nutmeg. Some may need to be ground or lightly crushed, others may be left whole, but do not overdo the amount. You could end up with your pot-pourri smelling like mincemeat.

When all of these ingredients are mixed together, you may add a little of any of the essential oils sold today for the purpose. Good quality oils only should be used if you wish for something better than the smell of boiled sweets. Do not use too much – a few drops will be enough, depending on quantity of dried material.

Storing
When the mixture is well stirred, pack into large jars; sweet jars with screw-top lids are ideal. Put one or two small bags of silica gel in each jar to absorb any moisture. Leave them in a cool, dark place for several weeks to mature.

✳ *HINT Silica gel bags can be used over and over again, if you dry them out occasionally in a low oven.*

Although the flower-petal pot-pourri is very pretty and can be kept fresh by the occasional addition of scented oils – and any bright petals whether scented or not – my favourite is made entirely with aromatic leaves.

Pot -pourri of aromatic leaves
Among the leaves I use are the following:
Lemon verbena (*Aloysia citriodora*)
Ginger mint (*Mentha gentilis*)
Peppermint (*Mentha piperita*)
Eau-de-Cologne-scented mint (*Mentha* 'Eau de Cologne')
Calamintha nepetoides (tiny blue flowers)
Thyme, various kinds
Marjoram (*Origanum vulgarea*)
Basil (*Ocimum basilicum*)
Pelargonium (half-hardy) leafy plants, rose and lemon scented, dried
Orange and lemon peel, dried
Sweet flag (*Acorus calamus*) rhizomes, dried and chopped

These all add up to make the longest-lasting scent. I also add a spice or lemon-scented oil and use dried marigold petals and soft-coloured forms of immortelles, like Helichrysum to add shape and colour to the glass fish-bowls where my leaf pot-pourri is kept, after several weeks of maturing in sealed jars. Often as I pass by, I put my hand into the jar to scrunch up the dried leaves. Even at a year old, the perfume they exude is strong and evocative, piercing and sublimating any additional oils I may have added.

The Maker
Beth Chatto is internationally known for her nursery and gardens in Essex where, over 30 years, she has made a collection of unusual hardy plants gathered from all around the temperate world. She is the author of the well-reviewed books: *The Dry Garden, The Damp Garden, Beth Chatto's Garden Notebook* and *The Green Tapestry.* Beth Chatto emphasises in her garden the need for plants to be grown in conditions similar to those in which they have been found in the wild.

Beth Chatto has been awarded 10 Gold Medals for exhibits at The Chelsea Flower Show and The Royal Horticultural Society.

Beth Chatto makes pot-pourri as a hobby only, and gives it as gifts to family and friends; it is not available commercially. Her recipes are a gift to you and this book.

Dry Pot-pourri

INGREDIENTS:
About 1.75 litres (3pt) mixed dried flowers and/or leaves
Whole and ground spices used sparingly
dried peel from 2 oranges or lemons
fixative: 42g (1.5oz) ground Orris root

Pot-pourri can be as variable as the plant material available. It should be as pretty as a flower arrangement, have a lingering perfume, and be offered in low bowls or round glass containers where it can be stirred occasionally by hand.

Moist Pot-Pourri

Take a large jar and pack layers of partially dried petals with sprinklings of salt, about 250ml (1 cup) salt to 500ml (2 cups) petals, well pressed down.

Other recipes use brandy or orange peel as a preservative. When well-made and kept in lidded containers the fragrance is retained much longer than using the dry method, but is more prone to failure and does not look so attractive.

Expense in making pot-pourri is minimal, and any work involved is more like pleasure. The time spent can fit in easily around other things. It sounds lovely. Why not try it?

FLOWERS BLOOM IN WOOD

by Percy Smith

These beautiful and unique Romany wooden flowers are probably unlike any you have ever seen, although they may remind you of big-balled chrysanthemums.
Everyone's flowers will look different. Some may turn out looking like sunflowers and be as big as a saucer, because every person has a different touch as they cut the petals.

Step-by-step instructions

MATERIALS:
pieces of elder, each about 25 1/2 cm (10in) in length, 2cm (3/4 in) width – larger or smaller depending on desired size of the 'flower head'
slight branches of privet OR crepe-covered wire (for the 'stem' of the flower)
very sharp knife (an open knife. Percy's was made from an old bread knife; the curved blade is about 7 1/2 cm [3in] long).
red and yellow dylon (cold water dye)

METHOD

1. Cut lengths of elder from trees in October, after the leaves have fallen from the elder.

2. Saw the elder into lengths of 25 1/2 cm (10in)

3. Use a sharp knife to take the bark off.

4. Hold the wood in one hand, and with a gentle action start to shave back the 'petals' with a very sharp knife. Draw the wood slightly towards you as you cut the petals. Twist the wood slightly and shave back another petal. This takes practice.

5. Continue cutting petals until the soft part of the wood is reached; at this point the flower head will drop off the end of the branch.

6. Dye them the traditional red or yellow, or any other colour you fancy in cold-water dye.

7. Leave the flower heads to dry, standing them on the stem end.

8. Make a small hole in the soft part of the wood of the flower head; push the flower head onto the sharpened end of a piece of freshly cut privet, leaving the leaves on. The privet leaves become the leaves of the flower.

9. Stand the branches in an inch or two of water to keep privet fresh.

Opposite: Pot-pourri, Ceramic Tile Planters and Romany Wooden Flowers

✳ HINT These Romany flowers are very strong. They can be washed and re-dyed.

The first step is to find a good source of elder. Choose branches carefully to preserve the shape of the bush. Percy can make a flower in less than a minute. But cutting the petals is a skill that will take time to learn, perhaps practising on and off over a week or two.

Once you do get the hang of it, you will be able to make memorable and individual flowers for yourself, for presents or for charity.

The Maker

Percy's first home was a painted horse-drawn wooden caravan on the moors of South Yorkshire. Favourite stopping-places were where they could find the raw materials for their crafts – willow, hazel and elder bushes – from which they fashioned flowers, pegs and baskets to sell, and near where the men could find casual labour on the farms.

When Percy was a lad of about 16, his dad taught him how to make these 'flower heads' as they were sitting around the open fire. He also taught him how to make dale pegs (from 'old window-frame wood' - deal), and pegs made from willow, which are easier to make, but don't last as long.

The flower heads were dyed the traditional red and yellow, probably from natural dyes like red berries and onion skins.

Then his mother put the flower heads in a wicker basket, and went out to sell them in the local town. People bought them for Christmas decorations, and to cheer up the house in winter. The Romany women made most of the wooden flowers (and the waxed crepe roses, page 59) and used them to decorate their own homes as well.

Those days are just a memory now. The craft is dying out, and Percy's children are not interested in learning how to do it.

This Romany family have very occasionally demonstrated how to make these flowers when, say, a teacher has made a request.

'If it helps' they are happy to give their distinctive flowers to *The Oxfam Make-a-Gift Book.*

Opposite: *'Bows and Roses' Decorated Egg, egg with cutting marks and a selection of Oppenheimer's Boxes*

GIFTS TO MAKE

♥♥♥♥♥♥♥♥♥♥♥♥♥♥♥♥♥♥♥♥♥

'BOWS AND ROSES' DECORATED EGG

by Joan Cutts

There is more than a hint of Fabergé-egg splendour here in this decorated goose egg. Elegant and fragile, the 'Bows and Roses' Decorated Egg, will bring a flash of turn-of-the-century Russia to your home. It can be used to hold a very special piece of jewellery.

Step-by-step instructions

MATERIALS:
blown egg: hen, duck or goose
egg stand (from craft shops)
braid
material for lining
pearls, plastic-type bought on a
  string, and/or more expensive
  rhinestones
small hinge (from ironmongers)
epoxy resin (fast set)
paint: enamel-type (eg. car spray or
  model-makers paint); emulsion;
  poster paint
PVA (ie, white craft glue that dries
  transparent)
thread
vaseline
needle
paintbrush, soft and good quality
hack-saw blade, junior (from
  ironmongers) OR *electric craft drill*
tweezers, fine
screwdriver, tiny flat
pencil
elastic bands

METHOD

How to blow an egg:
1. Leave the egg to reach room temperature
2. Use a large needle to puncture both ends; the pointed end is the easiest to do first. With a quick but gentle jerk, insert the needle. Turn the egg over and repeat the process. The hole at the blunt end must be slightly larger.
3. Shake the egg, then quickly blow in from the pointed end to expel contents.
4. Wash the egg; leave to dry.
5. Sandpaper the egg, if necessary, to remove any tiny bumps that sometimes exist on the shell.

Marking the egg for cutting:
Use a blown egg, preferably a goose egg, although a smaller one could be used.
   Remember that measurements will depend on the size of your egg.

1. Mark the egg into 6 equal sections. To do this, stretch three flat elastic bands lengthways over

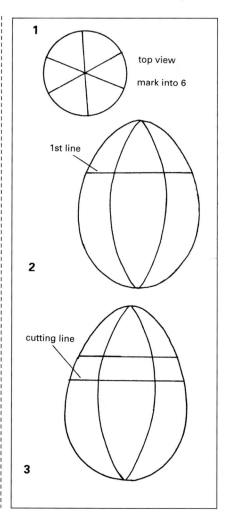

1
top view
mark into 6

1st line

2

cutting line

3

the egg; mark pencil lines down the side of the elastic bands, one used as a guide. (See diagram 1.)

2. Mark a line around the girth of the egg, halfway down the egg. (See diagram 2.)

3. Mark another line 5mm (about 1/4 in) below the last line around the girth.

● *NOTE   If the egg is small, that is a hen or duck egg, make the second line only 3mm (1/8 in) down. (See diagram 3.)*

4. Mark in the scallops (diagram 4), including double scallop for hinge (diagram 5). See also photograph page 39.

5. Mark in the bows. If you are using an electric craft drill to cut, you can cut the inside section of the bows out; otherwise, mark in and leave uncut. (See diagram 6.)

Cutting the egg:

1. Cut the scallop shape using an electric craft drill, if you have one.

OR

If you are a beginner:

a) Make your cutting line the second line you marked and cut it straight.

b) Using a blade from a junior hack-saw, score around the egg at the cutting line, that is the second line marked.

c) When using the hack-saw, you may have to score around 2 or 3 times until you feel the shell is cut.

2. Once cut, tidy the cut edges with a sharp knife, that is, clean edge of loose membrane.

Painting the egg:

Most types of paint can be used, except oil paint which takes too long to dry. Emulsion paint is good.

Use a good brush to avoid streaks in the finish. If the paint covers the bows you have drawn, just mark them in again.

1. Paint the inside of the egg as well as the outside to give extra strength.

2. Dry overnight.

3. Paint inside and out five more times.

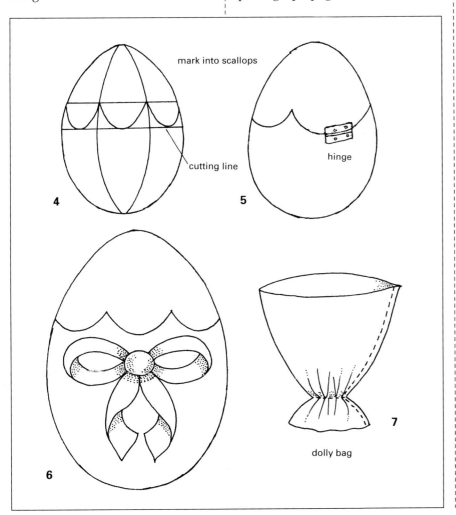

mark into scallops

cutting line

4

hinge

5

dolly bag

7

6

Lining the egg:
1. Measure the circumference of the open end of the eggshell, top and bottom sections.
2. Take a piece of material large enough to fit round, and sew up into a 'dolly-bag'. (See diagram 7.)
3. Glue this into the eggshells using PVA glue.
4. Add a pretty braid or lace to the top edge to hide the rough edges.

Applying the hinge:
1. First check whether the hinge should be loosened, as they are designed for wooden boxes; lever up the open flanges using a tiny flat screwdriver.
2. To prevent the epoxy resin from sealing the hinge, rub a tiny amount of vaseline into the middle bar.

✳ *HINT Do not get the vaseline anywhere near the area on which you will be placing the epoxy resin.*

3. You are now ready to apply the hinge. Hold the two sections of eggshell together using two elastic bands.
4. Scratch paint away from the area on which you will put the epoxy resin.
5. Mix the epoxy resin to maker's instructions and with great care place the glue on the egg. With great care lower the hinge onto the glue; fine tweezers will help.

● *NOTE Wait at least 10 minutes for the epoxy resin to dry before you try to open the egg.*

Outside decoration:
Using PVA glue, add the outside gold braid to outline the bows. (On the example illustrated, the inside of the bows were cut out and decorated with gold mesh from inside the egg, before the inside lining was inserted.)

Placing the egg on a stand:
Mix epoxy resin and apply it to the top of the stand. Place the egg in an upright position on the stand, and hold it for about 10 minutes.

✳ *HINT Rhinestones look lovely, but are quite expensive; plastic-type pearls on a string are a good substitute.*

Making the 'Bows and Roses' Decorated Egg is easy and inexpensive. It does require care and time – about 30 hours. This craft will bring beauty and fantasy into your home.

The Maker
Joan Cutts has been decorating eggs for 16 years. She is a professional who teaches her craft, has written articles about egg crafting for various magazines and colour supplements and speaks on the subject to interested groups. She is Life President and Founder of the Egg Crafters' Guild of Great Britain.

From its base in North Shields, Tyne and Wear, the Guild promotes interest in the decoration of eggs (other than those of protected species). The Guild, established in 1979, welcomes and helps its members enjoy this craft. A newsletter is published four times a year, and conventions, seminars and workshops are held throughout Britain. Membership includes 2,000 members in the UK and 60 groups overseas.

COLOURFUL PRINTED T-SHIRT

by Zarine Katrak

To celebrate Oxfam's 50th Anniversary, this design aims to reflect the idea that mutual understanding, respect and a will to work together can create unity – the basis for realistic growth and peaceful co-existence. With sponge printing and stencilling, the four colours of this flexible design are strikingly placed on a white background.

The design represents peoples of the world growing together in harmony, supportive of each other like the branches of a tree. It is the Tree of Life and an image of hope.

Step-by-step instructions

⬤ **NOTE** *Read through all instructions carefully (several times) before embarking on this design.*

MATERIALS:

Cotton T-shirt

pots of dye: black, red, yellow, blue and white, made up from Deka permanent colour paste OR Dylon colour fun fabric paint. Mix green from yellow and blue. The white is for any tiny spillages onto the work.

masking tape

cartridge paper, good quality

craft knife

sponge, synthetic, cut into cubes of about 2.5cm (1in) (Rinse and dry thoroughly.)

plastic glove, thin

paint brush, fine

indelible pen, fine and black

old sheet

magazine with quality of paper like that of the Radio Times *(glossy magazines are not absorbent enough)*

hair dryer

iron

ruler

pencils

scissors

needle and thread, OR sewing machine

METHOD

1. Prepare a flat table with a smooth, old double sheet (folded at least three times to give a slightly padded area to print on) and large enough to take the piece of fabric to be printed. Lay out all equipment.

2. Prepare fabric for printing by washing and rinsing thoroughly. DO NOT USE CONDITIONER.

⬤ **NOTE** *All finishes must be removed for dye to adhere.*

3. Place several sheets of the *Radio Times* inside body of T-shirt so dye will not seep through to the back.

⬤ **NOTE** *T-shirt MUST be cotton.*

4. Mask out the square or rectangle that will take the completed printing.

Think of this as the area where you will create a balanced picture.

5. Draw a linear representation of the blocks of background colour (as illustrated).

6. Cut each block to size and arrange on T-shirt according to the linear diagram.

Red square: 15.5 x 15cm
  (6 x 5 $^3/_4$ in)

Small green square: 15 x 8.5cm
  (5 $^3/_4$ x 3 $^1/_4$ in)

Blue square: 15 x 12.5cm
  (5 $^3/_4$ x 5in)

Yellow square: 35.5 x 15.25cm
  (14 x 6in)

Large green square: 29.5 x12.5cm
  (11 $^1/_2$ x 5in)

(Only two parts of this large green square 'show'. See illustration.)

Check that the size is accurate, and the composition balanced – trust your eye.

7. Remove all but the block to be printed in red. Stick strips of masking tape to the T-shirt to mark the edges of the block. Remove the block.

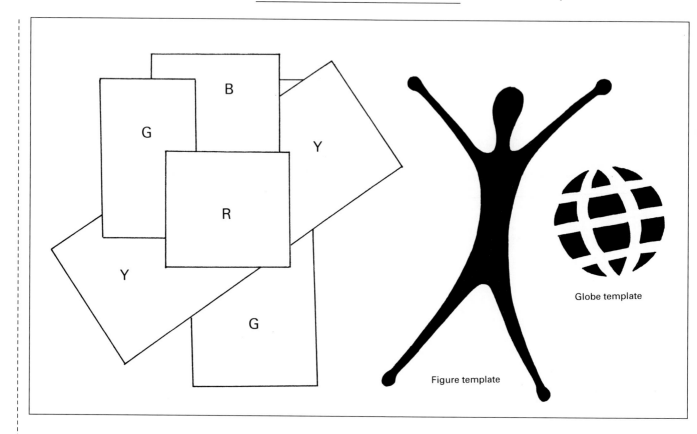

Globe template

Figure template

8. Drop a small quantity of dye onto a plastic lid (eg. ice-cream carton); pick up a tiny amount of dye on sponge, and on a clear section of the plastic lid use an up-and-down movement with the sponge, which will spread an even, thin layer of dye onto the sponge. Keep charging your sponge with dye througout the printing process, BUT be careful not to overload with dye.

✱ *HINT Experiment on scraps of material.*

9. Apply the charged sponge to your masked block, and cover it as evenly as you can. Watch out for any faint patches and go over these patches while the dye is still wet.

✱ *HINT Never attempt to 'touch up' when the fabric is dry, as it will just make dark, messy patches (except in the case of black dye).*

10. When you feel confident that your masked block is evenly covered, dry thoroughly with a hair dryer.

● **NOTE** *T-shirting, because of its ribbed texture, will not cover as evenly with a sponging technique, as it would with a printed technique. However, even if the finish is a little mottled, it is still pleasing to the eye, and has a hand-finished quality. If you do want a more 'perfect' finish, use a cotton or cotton satin panel for printing on; then sew it onto your garment.*

Opposite: *Colourful Printed T-shirt, A Bouquet of Roses*

11. Remove masking tape, and repeat process for all the other colour blocks. (See illustrations.)

12. Copy the (human) figure onto best-quality cartridge paper. Cut out carefully with a craft knife. Make two stencils.

13. Using the same sponging technique (as employed for the colour blocks), test out the stencil on a scrap of fabric. In between each print, blot the stencil at least three times on clean pages of a magazine like the *Radio Times* (more glossy magazines are not absorbent enough).

14. Between each print remember to blot the stencil and dry each print with a hair dryer.

15. OXFAM GLOBE: For the Oxfam globe, draw around a two-pence piece, and copy in the lines. If this seems too difficult, trace the logo and transfer onto the cartridge paper.

16. Using an indelible black pen with a fine nib, write 'Growth through Unity' on a piece of paper. Place under T-shirt and use as a guide to write the words.

● *NOTE This is actually quite difficult, as the fabric, being stretchy, moves. Again, test on a scrap of fabric, ideally an old cotton T-shirt.*

17. If the fabric is too thick to see through to the guide, practise writing freehand on your scrap of fabric. Then take the plunge and write directly onto the panel.

Alternatively, write it on a strip and sew this on, or use iron-on tape.

18. Don't forget to initial the finished piece of work.

19. Remove masking-tape frame.

20. Iron on reverse side of print according to manufacturer's instructions (for dyes as they relate to cotton) to fix the work.

21. Once fixed the fabric should be hand-washed and wrung, then allowed to drip dry. Iron while still damp on the reverse of the print.

22. WELL DONE!

This project will take 6 to 8 hours in all. The cost can vary greatly; it's up to you to decide how much you want to spend, on the fabric, for example. The techniques you will learn are simple, but require a careful, methodical approach. They will enable you to tackle smaller and larger projects, using colour and design to make your own creations.

The Maker

Zarine Katrak has been designing, printing and painting seriously since 1986. In her work, she uses silks, cottons and canvas to produce a wide range of work - from 1.75m (6ft) high, four-panel, oak-and-silk room-screens, and furnishing and garment fabric to small items of silk jewellery, bow-ties and bags.

Essentially, she puts dye on a natural fabric with a pre-determined composition in mind. Her inspiration is rooted in Indian art and design as well as being influenced by such western artists as Matisse, Kandinski and Le Corbusier.

She also spends time as a freelance trainer on specific health and social issues relating to women; in addition to voice and creative workshops, she believes that: 'empowerment is the key to an effective, fulfilled life. Using the creative and expressive arts can help individuals rediscover valuable resources within themselves that they may have thought lost.'

Zarine Katrak lives in mid-Wales with her partner and two children.

SOFT-AND-EASY PLAITED RUG

by Althea Tyndale

It is important for all of us, especially children, to learn how to recycle rubbish, to think about what we throw away, and to see how it can be transformed into something beautiful and useful. Learning to do these things with love can influence how we deal with people, too.

Plaiting is partnership made visible. It harmonises different colours and textures to produce a unified, beautiful and useful whole. The gift involves a reconsideration and reuse of what seems useless, unloved and unwanted in order to enjoy making something that will give pleasure and be useful to someone. Rag rugs are lovely and soft on the feet, as bedside rugs or in the bathroom. They wash and dry quickly and easily.

Step-by-step instructions

MATERIALS:

● **NOTE** *To make a circular rug about 1 metre (1 yard) across, you need about 1 1/2 to 2 carrier bags stuffed full of nylons/tights.*

old nylon stocking/tights OR strips of left-over cloth, useable bits from worn-out clothing, tea-towels, bedclothes and so on: 5cm (2in) wide.
thread
needles: one medium (for sewing strips together), one larger (for stitching plaits)
safety pin OR rubber band

✱ *HINT Tights: Don't mix thick winter weight and light summer weight – may make the surface uneven.*

METHOD

1. Take tights and cut off elastic waistbands and any seams, so you have a bundle of legs only.

2. Take any 3 and stitch ends together. This is the beginning of your plait.

3. Place the stitched ends under a heavy book or similar weight, and plait the 3 strands. If using cloth, tuck the raw ends under as you go.

4. When you come to the end of a strand, simply stitch on another leg (or cloth strip) and carry on plaiting. If the raw edge of the seam comes on top by mistake, just twist the stocking, so the seam edge lies underneath.

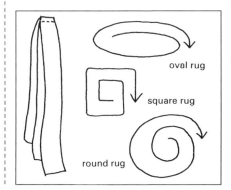

oval rug

square rug

round rug

5. When you've plaited about a metre (yard), fasten the loose ends of the plait together with a safety pin or a rubber band. Turn the plait the wrong side up, and start to coil it in the shape you want.

6. Starting from the centre and working outwards, stitch the coils together along the sides of the plait. It is best to use double thread, as this is stronger. You can take quite big, loose, untidy stitches – nobody is going to see them, and loose stitches are better

The Maker
I have been sewing since I was a little girl, and am now a semi-professional, teaching crafts and selling my work.
My grandmother made rag rugs to go under the sink and the stove to catch wet and greasy drips. There was always one on the go – she just added to the plait as a strip of cloth came to hand. The unplanned design was just as pleasing as a designed one.

than ones too tight. You can go over the back of the rug after it is completed, if you want, neatening up any really awkward places.

● *NOTE When the rug exceeds the size of your work-table, spread it on the floor and sew it up flat, so the tension stays even and 'waves' don't start to form.*

7. Just keep adding more nylons (or cloth strips) to your plait, and more plait to your rug, until you have the size you want.

8. To finish off, stitch the ends of the three strands together, and tuck under the bottom of the rug, keeping it as neat and flat as possible. Stitch firmly in place and fasten off thread securely.

✱ *HINT Try mixing fabrics, to give the rug colour and texture. The fabric 'weights' should be the same, though.*

You can work on this gift off and on, when it suits you. Depending on size, it may take around five hours to make. Best of all, it's free.

CELEBRATION CRACKERS AND GIFTS

by Tim Hunkin

The unique humour and talent of Tim Hunkin are themselves part of his Anniversary gifts. The Crackers, Skittles, Silhouettes, Hat Stand, Useful Car Stopper, High Speed Christmas Star, Bash the Rat, Magic Parcel, and Floor Polishing Shoes are quick and easy to make. They help recycle material, and give us a new way of looking at things and understanding them.

The Maker
Tim Hunkin is perhaps best known for his 'Rudiments of Wisdom' cartoons which appeared in the *Observer Magazine* (1973-87), and were then published in 1988 by Hamlyns as an encyclopedia, *Almost Everything There is to Know*. The quirky humour imparted knowledge to children and adults in an effective way.

His many talents and accomplishments include the following: author of a children's story, *Mrs Gronkwonk and the Post Office Tower*; maker of fireworks, staging displays and animated models, for example for Pink Floyd, and as theatre props; writer and illustrator of features for the *Observer Magazine*; creator of exhibitions - of wooden animals at the Craft's Council Gallery, 'The Disgusting Spectacle' exhibition of mechanical sculptures at the Institute of Contemporary Arts, the touring 'Art Gallery' exhibition; researching and writing television programmes – Q.E.D's 'Why Things Go Wrong', Channel 4's 'The Secret Life of Machines', and much more. He also designed and constructed both the water clock and the steam-powered clock for Neal's Yard, Covent Garden, and the wind-powered clock for the Liverpool Garden Festival.

In 1980 Tim Hunkin worked with Oxfam in Africa for two months.

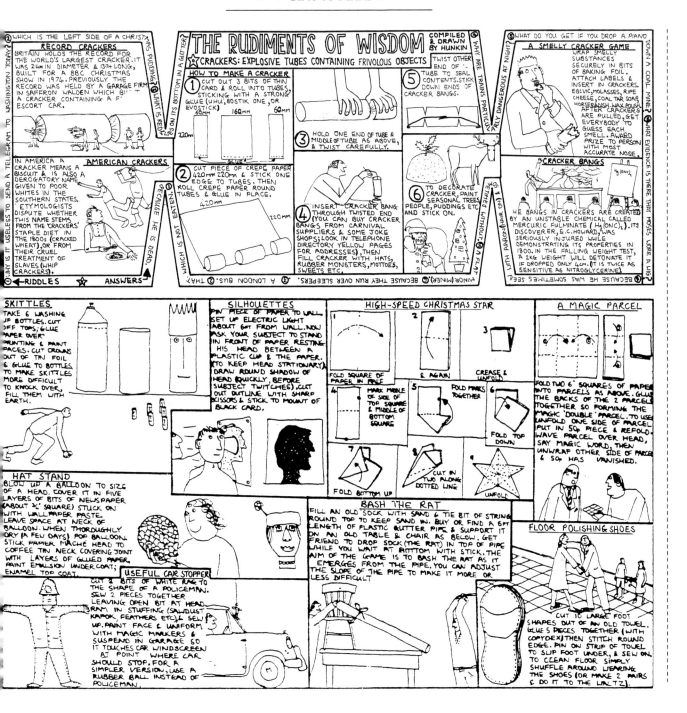

THE RUDIMENTS OF WISDOM

COMPILED & DRAWN BY HUNKIN

☆ CRACKERS: EXPLOSIVE TUBES CONTAINING FRIVOLOUS OBJECTS

② WHICH IS THE LEFT SIDE OF A CHRISTMAS PUDDING?

RECORD CRACKERS
BRITAIN HOLDS THE RECORD FOR THE WORLD'S LARGEST CRACKER. IT WAS 2¼m IN DIAMETER & 13¾m LONG, BUILT FOR A BBC CHRISTMAS SHOW IN 1974. PREVIOUSLY THE RECORD WAS HELD BY A GARAGE FIRM IN SAFFRON WALDEN WHICH BUILT A CRACKER CONTAINING A FORD ESCORT CAR.

AMERICAN CRACKERS
IN AMERICA A CRACKER MEANS A BISCUIT & IS ALSO A DEROGATORY NAME GIVEN TO POOR WHITES IN THE SOUTHERN STATES. ETYMOLOGISTS DISPUTE WHETHER THIS NAME STEMS FROM THE CRACKERS' STAPLE DIET IN THE 1900s (CRACKED WHEAT) OR FROM THEIR CRUEL TREATMENT OF SLAVES (WHIP CRACKERS).

←RIDDLES ☆ **ANSWERS→**

HOW TO MAKE A CRACKER
① CUT OUT 3 BITS OF THIN CARD & ROLL INTO TUBES, STICKING WITH A STRONG GLUE (UHU, BOSTIK ONE, OR EVOSTIK) 60MM 160MM 60MM 220MM GLUE

② CUT PIECE OF CREPE PAPER 420MM 220MM & STICK ONE EDGE TO TUBES, THEN ROLL CREPE PAPER ROUND TUBES & GLUE IN PLACE. 420MM 220MM

③ HOLD ONE END OF TUBE & MIDDLE OF TUBE AS ABOVE, & TWIST CAREFULLY.

④ INSERT CRACKER BANG THROUGH TWISTED END (YOU CAN BUY CRACKER BANGS FROM CARNIVAL SUPPLIERS & SOME JOKE SHOPS; LOOK IN TELEPHONE DIRECTORY YELLOW PAGES FOR ADDRESSES) THEN FILL CRACKER WITH HATS, RUBBER MONSTERS, MOTTOES, SWEETS ETC.

⑤ TWIST OTHER END OF TUBE TO SEAL CONTENTS. STICK DOWN ENDS OF CRACKER BANGS.

⑥ TO DECORATE CRACKER, PAINT SEASONAL TREES PEOPLE, PUDDINGS ETC AND STICK ON.

⑥ WHAT DO YOU GET IF YOU DROP A PIANO DOWN A COAL MINE?

A SMELLY CRACKER GAME
WRAP SMELLY SUBSTANCES SECURELY IN BITS OF BAKING FOIL. ATTACH LABELS & INSERT IN CRACKERS. EG: VIC, MOLASSES, RIPE CHEESE, COAL TAR SOAP HORSERADISH, WAX POLISH. AFTER CRACKERS ARE PULLED, GET EVERYBODY TO GUESS EACH SMELL. AWARD PRIZE TO PERSON WITH MOST ACCURATE NOSE.

CRACKER BANGS
THE BANGS IN CRACKERS ARE CREATED BY AN UNSTABLE CHEMICAL CALLED MERCURIC FULMINATE ($Hg(ONC)_2$). ITS DISCOVERER, E.C. HOWARD, WAS SERIOUSLY INJURED WHILE DEMONSTRATING ITS PROPERTIES IN 1800, IN THE FALLING WEIGHT TEST, A 2KG WEIGHT WILL DETONATE IT IF DROPPED ONLY 4CM. (IT IS TWICE AS SENSITIVE AS NITROGLYCERINE.)

SKITTLES
TAKE 6 WASHING UP BOTTLES. CUT OFF TOPS, GLUE PAPER OVER OPENING & PAINT FACES. CUT CROWNS OUT OF TIN FOIL & GLUE TO BOTTLES TO MAKE SKITTLES MORE DIFFICULT TO KNOCK OVER, FILL THEM WITH EARTH.

HAT STAND
BLOW UP A BALLOON TO SIZE OF A HEAD. COVER IT IN FIVE LAYERS OF BITS OF NEWSPAPER (ABOUT ¾" SQUARE) STUCK ON WITH WALLPAPER PASTE. LEAVE SPACE AT NECK OF BALLOON. WHEN THOROUGHLY DRY (A FEW DAYS) POP BALLOON. STICK PAPIER MACHE HEAD TO COFFEE TIN NECK COVERING JOINT WITH LAYERS OF GLUED PAPER. PAINT EMULSION UNDERCOAT; ENAMEL TOP COAT.

USEFUL CAR STOPPER
CUT 2 BITS OF WHITE RAG TO THE SHAPE OF A POLICEMAN. SEW 2 PIECES TOGETHER LEAVING OPEN BIT AT HEAD. CRAM IN STUFFING (SAWDUST, KAPOK, FEATHERS ETC) & SEW UP. PAINT FACE & UNIFORM WITH MAGIC MARKERS & SUSPEND IN GARAGE SO IT TOUCHES CAR WINDSCREEN AT POINT WHERE CAR SHOULD STOP. FOR A SIMPLER VERSION, USE A RUBBER BALL INSTEAD OF POLICEMAN.

SILHOUETTES
PIN PIECE OF PAPER TO WALL. SET UP ELECTRIC LIGHT ABOUT 6FT FROM WALL. NOW ASK YOUR SUBJECT TO STAND IN FRONT OF PAPER RESTING HIS HEAD BETWEEN A PLASTIC CUP & THE PAPER. (TO KEEP HEAD STATIONARY) DRAW ROUND SHADOW OF HEAD (QUICKLY, BEFORE SUBJECT TWITCHES). CUT OUT OUTLINE WITH SHARP SCISSORS & STICK TO MOUNT OF BLACK CARD.

HIGH-SPEED CHRISTMAS STAR
1 FOLD SQUARE OF PAPER IN HALF
2 & AGAIN
3 CREASE & UNFOLD
4 MARK MIDDLE OF SIDE OF TOP SQUARE & MIDDLE OF BOTTOM SQUARE
5 FOLD MARKS TOGETHER
6 FOLD TOP DOWN
7 FOLD BOTTOM UP
8 CUT IN TWO ALONG DOTTED LINE
UNFOLD

BASH THE RAT
FILL AN OLD SOCK WITH SAND & TIE BIT OF STRING ROUND TOP TO KEEP SAND IN. BUY OR FIND A 6FT LENGTH OF PLASTIC GUTTER PIPE & SUPPORT IT ON AN OLD TABLE & CHAIR AS BELOW. GET FRIEND TO DROP SOCK (THE RAT) IN TOP OF PIPE WHILE YOU WAIT AT BOTTOM WITH STICK. THE AIM OF THE GAME IS TO BASH THE RAT AS IT EMERGES FROM THE PIPE. YOU CAN ADJUST THE SLOPE OF THE PIPE TO MAKE IT MORE OR LESS DIFFICULT.

A MAGIC PARCEL
FOLD TWO 6" SQUARES OF PAPER INTO PARCELS AS ABOVE. GLUE THE BACKS OF THE 2 PARCELS TOGETHER SO FORMING THE MAGIC 'DOUBLE' PARCEL. TO USE UNFOLD ONE SIDE OF PARCEL, PUT IN SQ PIECE & REFOLD. WAVE PARCEL OVER HEAD, SAY MAGIC WORD, THEN UNWRAP OTHER SIDE OF PARCEL & SQ HAS VANISHED.

FLOOR POLISHING SHOES
CUT 10 LARGE FOOT SHAPES OUT OF AN OLD TOWEL. GLUE 5 PIECES TOGETHER (WITH COPYDEX) THEN STITCH ROUND EDGE. PIN ON STRIP OF TOWEL TO SLIP FOOT UNDER, & SEW ON. TO CLEAN FLOOR SIMPLY SHUFFLE AROUND WEARING THE SHOES (OR MAKE 2 PAIRS & DO IT TO THE WALTZ).

49

OPPENHEIMER'S BOX

from Nick Robinson for the British Origami Society

Paper has been with us for around 2,000 years, and paper-folding must be nearly as old. Developed primarily by the Japanese, origami is now an activity enjoyed universally. The reason for this popularity? Sharing.
Since it became popular in North America and Britain in the 1950s, great technological advances have been made and spread around the world by unselfish and talented folders. They want only to give others the pleasure they experienced whilst folding, a philosophy that has come to characterise paper-folders everywhere. They are united by a common aim: no less than to have the whole world folding paper and thus end all wars. This is made possible by using a common set of symbols in origami diagrams, so that all problems of language disappear and ideas and friendship can flow freely.
Many folders use recyled paper and see origami as a spiritual activity, as well as a practical one. By breathing new life into the paper, origami shows respect for the immense natural forces that caused the tree to grow in the first place.
Whether used as a container for a present or as a present in its own right, this piece of origami, named after its creator American Lillian Oppenheimer, is a gesture of friendship and the sharing of a simple skill.

Step-by-step instructions

MATERIAL:
paper, new or recycled

METHOD
Start with a rectangle: almost any size and shape will be fine. The facing side will be the inside of the box, and the underside the outside. Arrange the coloured side of your paper accordingly, with a long side towards you.

1. Start by folding the paper in half, so that the 2 longer edges meet each other. Make sure the edges are neatly lined up. Crease firmly and unfold.

2. Fold each longer edge into the central crease you have just made. Crease firmly and unfold again.
3. Rotate the paper so that a shorter edge is nearest you. Fold in half, as in step 1. Unfold again.
4. As in step 2, fold the short edges to meet on the central crease. This time, leave them in place.
5. You can see three creases running vertically across the paper. Place your finger just inside one of the quarter creases and swing the corner inwards so that it lies along the crease.

● **NOTE** *The corner should* NOT *meet the central edges.*

Check the next diagram if you are not sure.

6. This is how it should look Repeat the move on the three remaining corners.
7. Fold one of the central flaps back outwards as far as it will comfortably go; it should overlap the corners to some extent, depending on the shape of your initial sheet of paper.
8. This is the result. Repeat for the other central flap. This fold 'locks' the box together, so make the crease a firm one.

✴ *HINT This is the best way to store the box or to send it in the post.*

9. To open out, insert your fingers in between the central layers, and gently ease them apart. As they

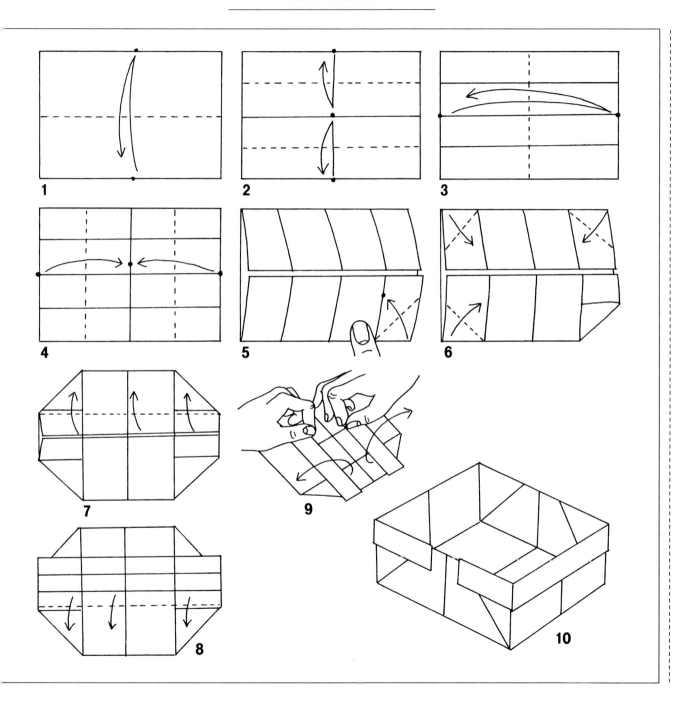

The Contributor
The British Origami Society (BOS) aims to develop and encourage Origami (folding paper) as a form of art, education, therapy and recreation. This amateur group, formed in 1967, publishes a bi-monthly magazine called *British Origami*, as well as booklets on the work of creative paper folders and on historical research. They have conventions twice a year and many smaller, informal meetings.

open, use your fingers to open and shape the box.

10. Make the box more attractive by gently pinching each corner edge between finger and thumb. Sharpen any other creases as well, if you wish.

Your first attempt may be a little messy, so try it again.

✱ *HINTS*
1. Experiment with different sizes, shapes, colours and types of paper.
2. Make large boxes or tiny ones (once you understand the folding principle).
3. Make a series of different sizes and slot them into each other.

Folding a lid:
To fold a lid, alter steps 2 and 4, so that the edges don't quite meet the central crease. A gap of lcm(3/8 in) is sufficient. Otherwise the folding method is the same. This will produce a box slightly longer and wider than the first - ideal as a lid.

Origami creation is often based around experimentation or 'doodling'. If you have any ideas whist folding the box, try them out. You can't break anything, and you may discover a new fold. (If you do, why not send it to the BOS?)

Oppenheimer's Box will ensure that you are never short of a gift box again.

The Maker
Nick Robinson has been involved with paper-folding for ten years. Along with many other members of BOS, he teaches origami in hospitals and schools, at libraries, youth clubs, colleges, speakers groups and to anyone interested.

He has written a book, *Paper Airplanes*, and regularly contributes to the BOS magazine. His original work has been published in 12 countries around the world.

THE OXFAM RAG RUG

by Jenni Stuart-Anderson

*Using the Oxfam globe logo, and four of the anniversary colours, this rug is a colourful, durable and useful gift.
The rag rug was once only for the cold floors of the poor. With the Industrial Revolution mill-woven fabric
became more available. As a result rags were hooked and prodded – 'progging' – through hessian sacks using
dolly pegs or hooks fashioned from nails or whatever came to hand. There were regional design variations, but
usually rugs were a random assortment of dull colours with, perhaps, a bit of red flannel. At the same time,
settlers in America were hooking rag rugs depicting scenes from their daily lives, with flowers and pets as a
favourite theme – now prized by collectors.
The rag rug often re-emerges during time of hardship, as it did during the last war, when rugs were prodded in
shelters, in the dark.
In the l980s, with the affluence and interest in recycling, the craft revived once again - this time as a colourful
means of self-expression.*

Step-by-step instructions

MATERIALS FOR A RUG 71CM (2¹/₃FT)
IN DIAMETER:

pens, coloured
fat felt marker pen OR crayon
paper (for trying different colour
    combinations, using pens and
    markers)
clothing OR blankets, recycled, dyed,
    if necessary in 4 colours (red,
    yellow, green, black), cut into pieces
    (See under Method.)
hessian, piece of 10oz common hessian
    OR sack, about 1m x lm (1yd x
    1yd) (unpicked round sides), fairly
    loose weave is best
tool to poke or pull, improvised (eg.
    large heavy tweezers OR pointed
    stick the size of a pencil OR forceps)
straightedge or something similar
scissors
needle and stout thread

OPTIONAL
(if you are dying fabric):
*For every 450g (1lb) of dry weight
    woollen blanket, you need 2 tins of
    Dylon. (Other makes of dye may
    colour different amounts of fabric.)*

● **NOTE** *See photograph of the
Oxfam Rag Rug on title page .*

METHOD

● **NOTE** *'Progging' is pushing or
pulling the cut strips of rag through
the hessian*

DIMENSIONS OF THE RUG:
globe - 59cm (23 ¹/₄ in) diameter
outer ring - 6cm (2 ¹/₄ in) wide,
progged area (globe + outer ring) –
71cm (27 ³/₄ in) diameter
hem - 5cm (2in) wide
*(rug + hem diameter = 81cm [31
³/₄ in])*

l. Make several copies or tracings
of the Oxfam globe logo. Try
different combinations of the
colours, by colouring them in on
paper to see which colours look
best.
2. If necessary, dye fabric in the 4
Oxfam Anniversary colours (red,
green yellow, black), one colour
per dying session.
3. To transfer the globe logo onto
the hessian:
a) Photocopy the globe and scale
up by multiplying the dimensions
by the number of times you are
increasing the size, and then draw
the curves by eye.
OR
Photocopy the symbol and have it
enlarged: the example illustrated
is 59cm (23 ¹/₄ in) diam., taping all
the photocopies together.

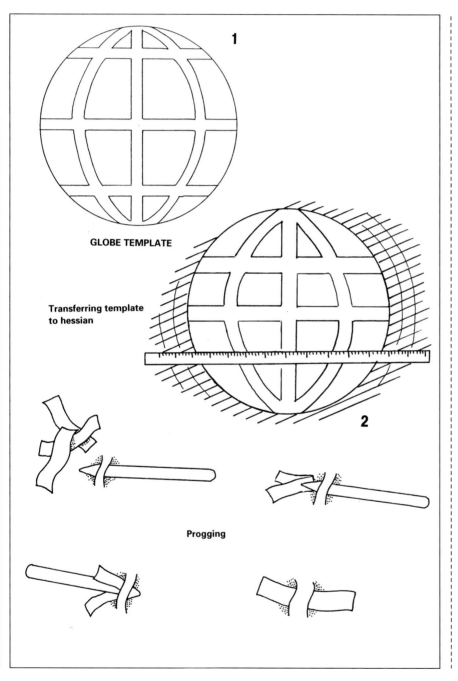

1

GLOBE TEMPLATE

Transferring template
to hessian

2

Progging

b) Trace the lines of one quarter of the globe and cut round the outside curved line to make a kind of template.

c) Place the photocopy or enlarged globe on top of a piece of hessian, large enough to leave an 11cm (4 $^1/_3$ in) border all round.

d) Using thin nail or picture pin, nail through centre of paper and hessian. Tie nail to one end of string and felt marker to the other end to make a rough compass.

e) Using the 'compass' draw on hessian: one circle to be outer edge of globe, one circle 6cm (2 $^1/_3$ in) outside it to mark edge of rug, and final circle 5cm (2in) outside that to give border, which will be turned under and hemmed as a final step.)

f) Place straightedge on top of globe logo and mark at the edge of the paper, on the hessian, where the straight lines come (see diagram 2).

g) Lift paper (enlargement of globe) off and mark straight lines in with straightedge.

h) Place tracing over one-quarter of globe, matching centres. Use as a template to draw in curved lines. Repeat on other three segments.

4. Progging the rags:

a) Cut strips of fabric 7.5cm (3in) wide, as long as you like, cutting with the weave, not bias cut.

Opposite: Puppet Rooster, Easy Desk Tidy, Soft-and-Easy Plaited Rug

54

b) Chop these strips into pieces about 12mm (^{1}/$_2$ in) wide for woollen fabric, and 2.5cm (1in) wide for cotton.

c) Work on segment of the globe, outlining it first, then filling in with the same colour.

'PROGGING':

i) Poke the tool (stick) through the hessian, as though making a stitch with a needle, making two holes about 1cm (^{1}/$_2$ in) apart, along the segment outline. Extract tool.

ii) Using the tool, push corner of rag piece through, pulling with fingers until the ends poke up evenly.

✳ *NOTE If using cotton fabric, pull two bits through at once to make it thicker.*

iii) 'Stitch' along drawn line: Poke tool into hessian, so that it exits through last hole it came out of, so each hole will have two bits of fabric poking out of it. The 'stitches' (lines of bits of rag) are worked in parallel lines about lcm (^{1}/$_2$ in) apart.

5. When a segment of the globe has been worked in one colour, work the adjacent lines in the next colour, working your way across the globe.

6. On the example illustrated, there are three rows of green for the main axes, and two rows for the other lines. The perimeter of the globe has one line only.

7. Finally, turn the raw edge under at the back of the rug, pin, and hem stitch using stout thread.

✳ *HINT This rug can be vacuumed or beaten, and hand-washed occasionally using non-detergent soap. Dry thoroughly after washing, as hessian will rot if left damp.*

● **NOTE** *The Oxfam Rag Rug is shown on the title page.*

The Oxfam Rag Rug may cost you nothing, only your time – 15 hours or less – but you will have a rug that will last forever.

The Maker
I trained and worked as an architectural and interior designer. After the birth of my daughter, I felt a real need to do something other than housework and child care. I asked a Herefordshire woman who had been rag-rug making for more than 50 years to show me her traditional techniques. After that I was hooked!

Now my daughter is in school, I still do some architectural work, but I find lots of interest in my rag-rug making workshops, now that recycling is of general interest. I also make rugs to commission, mainly hooked rugs, which are often 'pictures'. My rugs are in America, Canada, Italy, France nd New Zealand, as well as the U.K.

I am a member of the Association of Rag Rug Makers, the Hereford Society of Craftsmen, the Herefordshire Guild of Weavers, Spinners and Dyers and I am a Women's Institute tutor.

EASY DESK TIDY

by Pam Redwood for Squirrel Services

This useful gift is a handsome container for letters, papers, pens and pencils, and can be either free-standing or fixed to the wall. The Easy Desk Tidy can be personalised specially for whoever will use it. Taking the time to make this simple gift, rather than buying one, conveys to someone that you really care about them and the environment. Adding a message, such as 'Letters', 'Recipes', 'I'm Tidy', 'Congratulations' or 'I Love You', becomes part of the decoration.

This is an appropriate gift for Oxfam's Anniversary because we all need to take time to reuse and recyle wherever possible. The throw-away mentality is doing irreparable damage to our planet. Resist the ever-present advertisements to spend, spend, spend, and avoid buying excessively packaged goods whenever possible. We can learn a valuable lesson from other cultures who live more in tune with their environment.

Step-by-step instructions

MATERIALS:
cardboard boxes OR plastic boxes and cartons, empty (and free)
greeting cards, used OR Oxfam gift-wrapping paper
paper: plain OR coloured
Stanley knife
scissors
pens and pencils, coloured
paper
glue, prittstick OR copydex
glue (water-based)
sellotape
OPTIONAL:
plastic film, sticky-bucked

METHOD
1. Take some time to think about how you can personalise this gift for the recipient (hobbies or sports they enjoy). Also, remember the intended use will determine its shape and size.

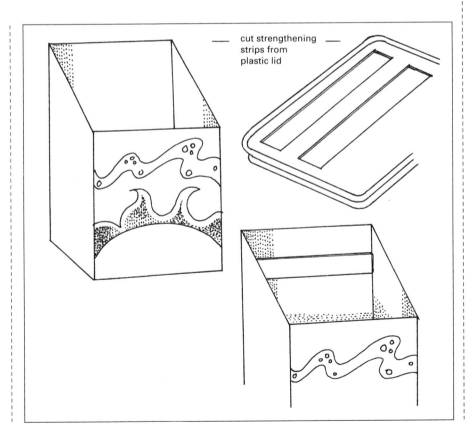

cut strengthening strips from plastic lid

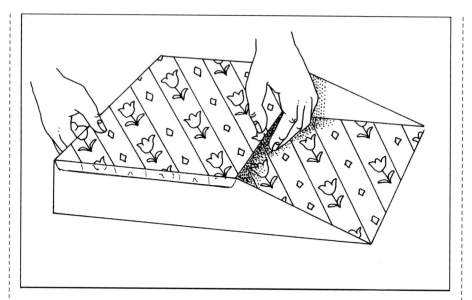

The Maker
Pam Redwood and her husband Peter run Norwich's most environmentally friendly business. Started in 1990, their business supplied products in refillable/deposit containers, the packaging accepted back for reuse or recycling. They operated a free home-delivery service using bicycles towing trailers.

Then the business moved to commercial premises. The shop offers products that are made by less energy-intensive processes and that help save finite resources. Amongst their range are recycled stationery, much of it made from post-consumer waste; energy-saving items such as low-energy light bulbs and rechargeable batteries (accepted back for recycling when they eventually wear out); and items that run on renewable energy such as solar-powered battery chargers, outdoor lighting, panels to heat water and small wind chargers.

The couple's main aim will always be the promotion of alternatives to polluting products.

2. Select the container in the size you need, and cut it down, using a Stanley knife. See diagrams.
3. If necessary, cut strengthening strips from flexible plastic.
4. Glue strips onto cardboard in areas of potential stress, using copydex glue.

✱ *HINT If you intend the container to be wall-mounted, strengthen that area so the screws will be well-supported.*

5. Choose the decorative paper and/or picture that will cover the container. Cut out to fit.
6. Glue pieces in place with a water-based glue. Smooth down any air bubbles.
7. Use your coloured pens and pencils to write your message, eg. 'I'm Tidy', and glue it on the container.

✱ *HINT To get rid of large air bubbles, puncture with a pin.*

8. Dry thoroughly.
9. A nice finishing touch to strengthen and enhance the gift, is a covering of sticky-backed plastic. Find another pair of hands to help you, as applying it can be tricky.

● *NOTE There are lots of variations on this idea. How about a spice rack made from plastic ice-cream cartons, and filled with Oxfam spices?*

The Easy Desk Tidy can be made in as little as half an hour. The more you make, the easier it becomes. Even better, you may begin to look at other ways of recycling material in your home.

A BOUQUET OF ROSES

by Alfreda Smith

Red and yellow are the traditional Romany colours for these beautiful waxed 'roses'. They are easy to make, but require care and some skill, which comes with practice. This contribution symbolises the Romany love of the natural world, a world we all need and enjoy. This world now needs our protection.

Step-by-step instructions

MATERIALS:

crepe paper
knife: an old pliable one is best (like old bone-handled knives)
scissors
candle, white
wire, lightweight
privet, freshly cut branches OR crepe-covered wire

METHOD

1. Cut a strip of crepe paper 60 x 13cm (24 x 5in) with the grain running as shown in the diagram.
2. Fold the strip in half, and in half again two more times, so there are 8 sections ('petals'). Trim the corners. 'Petals' stay in strip form.
3. Place crepe on knee. Place knife on top of petal. Curl back the top edge of each 'petal', by drawing the knife toward you.

✳ HINT *Don't wear slippery material when you are working with the crepe on your knee.*

4. Turn the crepe over, and with your thumbs stretch the body of the 'petal' into a bowl shape.
5. Wind the strip of tissue paper round the fingers of one hand – not too tightly – so that the 'petals' will curl out and you will get a full-blown flower.
6. Slide the rolled paper off your fingers and twist the bottom of the roll. Secure with wire, and tie to a length of freshly cut privet.
7. Melt a candle in a saucepan.
8. Carefully dip the ends of the petals into the wax. When they are completely coated, gently lift out, and rest on paper to let the excess wax drip off, but not for long, or they will stick!
9. Place in a jar or a vase to dry, making sure they don't touch each other.

The Romany wax 'roses' are basically easy to make. The skill will come with practice and experimentation.

The Maker
Alfreda learned to make these waxed crepe flowers a long time ago by watching her mother make them. She used to create the shaved wooden flowers too (see 'Flowers Bloom in Wood', p.36), until her hands were no longer strong enough. Alfreda grew up in a wooden caravan. Now she lives in a house, and hopes that making flowers will keep her arthritis at bay. She still goes out with her bouquets of waxed roses, and likes to meet again the friends she has made over so many years.

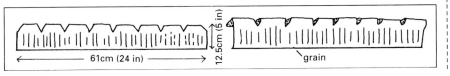

61cm (24 in)   12.5cm (5 in)   grain

PUPPET ROOSTER

by Jessica and Jenny Bryne-Daniel for Designers of Distinction

Follow the movements of this enthralling toy with your eyes. Puppets have entertained both children and adults for centuries. This one is easy to make as a gift or for yourself. Have you ever wondered how a puppet is made? Here's how.

Step-by-step instructions

MATERIALS:

6 wooden balls OR papier mâché balls: one about 4.5cm (1 3/4 in) diam. for body; one 3.5cm (1 1/2 in) diam. for head; one 3cm (1 1/4 in) diam. for neck; one 2.5cm (1in) diam. for tail-piece; two 2cm (3/4in) diam. for feet. All approximate measurements. (See illustration)

beads, small ready-threaded, for legs

4 red beads, to use to tie-off nylon threads through batten

nylon thread, 3m (10ft)

tail feathers, if possible small cockerel tail feathers

paint for eyes and beak

red tin foil (could be from candy wrappers) OR modern red plastic modelling strips OR strips of red fabric, to make the comb

thick wire covered in modern plastic strips OR strips of fabric, for feet

varnish for wooden balls OR paint for papier mâché balls

household drill

wire cutter

wood for batten and bar: both 1cm (1/4 in) square; batten 22.5cm (8 3/4 in) long; bar 16.5cm (6 1/2 in) long

METHOD

1. Drill one hole through each of the balls.
2. Varnish/paint all balls. Dry.
3. Thread the four largest balls loosely onto piece of nylon thread.
4. Make the comb.
5. Make the beak from cardboard, painted, or black plastic.
6. Paint/glue on the eyes, beak, comb.
7. Drill a hole and insert the tail feathers, gluing with strong glue.
8. Form the feet by cutting and shaping wire for three talons and a spur for each foot. Wrap wire with modern plastic modelling strips or strips of fabric. Insert wires in each wooden bead 'foot'.
9. Make legs, each approx. 7.5cm (3in) long.
10. Suspend by attaching nylon thread to the head and tail, and approx. half-way along the legs.
11. Make the batten and bar: where they cross, 1/2 house the two battens, so they fit together smoothly OR nail OR glue together. Drill a small hole near the end of each piece, where the nylon thread can be taken through to be tied off with a bead.
12. Attach the other end of the four suspending nylon threads to the wood batten and bar.
13 Balance the bird by adjusting the length of the suspending nylon threads. Enjoy getting to know the rooster's movements.

✱ *HINT A variety of puppets can be made using the simple method above.*

The Puppet Rooster has irresistible charm. It is suprisingly easy and inexpensive to make.

The Makers
Jessica and Jenny Bryne-Daniel run a young design practice in Gwynedd, Wales, where they create original designs combining the ancient arts of calligraphy, illumination, embroidery and other textile techniques. They specialise in highly personal work into which they incorporate many references to the client, thereby creating unique items that have a lasting quality, becoming family treasures and heirlooms.

Opposite: *Sewing Jewel, Traveller's Emergency Kit.*

GIFTS TO SEW

♥♥♥♥♥♥♥♥♥♥♥♥♥♥♥♥♥♥♥

SEWING JEWEL

by Elaine Hammond for Patchwork & Quilting Magazine

This charming little jewel of a present is a variation on an old Victorian pin-cushion idea. As a patchwork pin-cushion, it is an attractive aid to any seamstress. Round the outside are strung eight reels of sewing cotton – always to hand – the colours enhancing this pretty item.
This gift recycles and is almost free, because most, if not all, of the materials can be pretty scraps. If you live in the country, you may be able to find the stuffing by gathering lambswool from fences! It can be easily made in the Oxfam Anniversary colours.

Step-by-step instructions

MATERIALS:

cotton, polycotton or velvet scraps
   (i.e., in 3 coordinating fabrics)
stuffing (old tights OR lambswool
   OR polyester wadding OR kapok
   OR bran)
card, thin (birthday cards or
   postcards)
card (cereal packet)
card, thicker (for template D)
thread, matching fabric colours (for
   sewing)
glue, UHU
ribbon, toning, 1m (1yd) of 12mm
   (1/2 in) wide
needle
scissors
awl OR paper punch

AS PART OF GIFT:

8 reels of cotton, in a variety of
   colours
needles, packet
pins

METHOD

● **NOTE** *This gift can be simplified by omitting the patchwork on top. It can be made more difficult by increasing the complexity of the patchwork design.*

1. From thin card, cut 1 template A and 8 template B.
2. From cereal card, cut 8 template C.
3. From thickest card, cut 1 template D.
4. Cut fabric for each template, allowing 5cm (1/4 in) seam allowance. Tack the fabric around templates A and B to sew in the English method (see diagram A), but use glue to stick the fabric around templates C and D.
5. Oversew template A and B pieces together on the wrong side (diagram B).
6. Remove the card from A and B pieces.
7. Bend the covered template C pieces at both ends along the line shown, then oversew these 8

The Maker
Elaine Hammond has always been interested in craft. She experimented with a variety of crafts, until she discovered patchwork and quilting in her late teens. She has been very keen ever since. In 1985, with Dianne Huck, she started *Patchwork & Quilting* magazine, of which she is co-editor.
   In 1989 the first Quilts UK was held at the Three Counties Showground at Malvern, Worcestershire, organised by Elaine and Dianne and their husbands. Thousands of visitors view the hundreds of quilts on display.

TEMPLATES

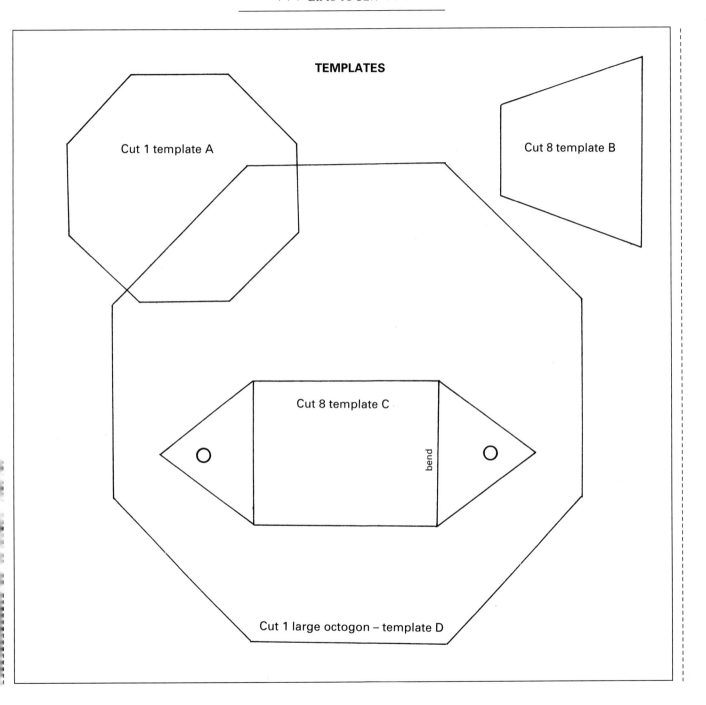

Cut 1 template A

Cut 8 template B

Cut 8 template C

bend

Cut 1 large octogon – template D

63

pieces to the completed top, finishing by oversewing the points on the outside.

8. Now oversew 6 edges of the template D piece to the completed top on the outside, and then stuff firmly before stitching the 2 final seams.

9. Using an awl or a paper punch, make holes in the points as shown on template C.

10. Thread the ribbon through the first hole, through a cotton reel, then through the second hole and so on. Finish with a bow.

Enjoy your pin-cushion! It costs almost nothing, and may take eight to twelve hours (or about three evenings) to make. This fine and useful item makes a perfect present.

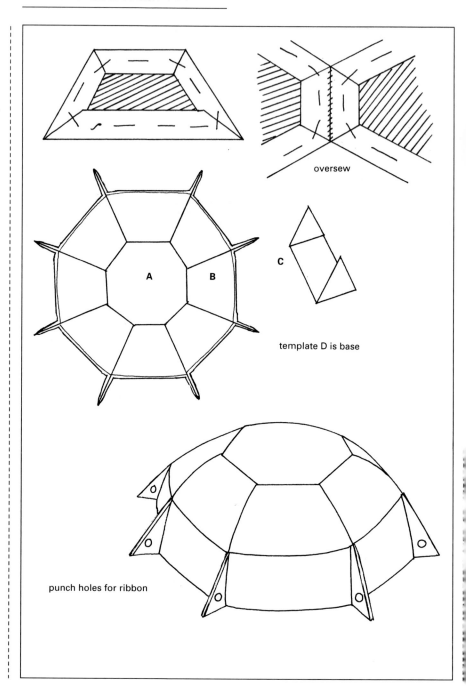

oversew

A   B

C

template D is base

punch holes for ribbon

KNITTED TOYS

by Jane Platt for the Knitting & Crochet Guild

*Mr Kroak the Frog and Children round the World are knitted toys to charm both knitter and child.
And they are fun to knit.*

ABBREVIATIONS:

cm	centimetre(s)
DK	double knitting
P	purl
g	gram(s)
K	knit
st(s)	stitches
mm	millimetre(s)
st.st	stocking stitch, K-side is right side
in	inch(es)
g.st	garter stitch, every row K
rem	remaining
rev.st.st	reversed stocking stitch, P-side is right side
tog	together
beg	beginning

MR KROAK THE FROG

Mr Kroak was originally inspired by a photograph of a tropical tree frog, with its long, thin body and limbs straddling two branches, bulging eyes and rather funny appearance. This frog, Mr Kroak, takes these features to a ridiculous extreme – relaxed in his bean bag, yet with an air of sophistication in his bow tie, and collar and cuffs. He is easy to make, knitted in stocking stitch in rectangular pieces, so no shaping is required. His body is decorated with an all-over simple Fair Isle pattern in bright and mint green with ribbon and surface embroidery.

Mr Kroak is knitted in the Oxfam Anniversary colours, and in his own special way is based on a creature which originates in an area helped by Oxfam.

● *NOTE*
*Size of completed item, sitting in bean-bag: 19cm (7 1/2in) high
Mr Kroak, head to toe: 30cm (12in)*

MATERIALS:
Yarn
    Yarn in example illustrated is 100% acrylic.
Bean-bag: 50g (2oz) yellow double knitting (A)
Frog: 15g (1/2 oz) bright green 4ply (B)
Body pattern: oddment pale green 4ply (C)

● **NOTE** *All amounts are approximate, and may vary according to the yarn used.*

TRIMMINGS:
pair goo-goo eyes: 25mm (1in)

*ribbon bow: 7mm (1/4 in) for bow-tie ribbon, wide: 25.5cm (10in) in length for collar and cuffs
length of yarn, red and dark green OR embroidery thread for nostrils and mouth detail
yarn, black, OR embroidery thread for waistcoat and button detail
thread, fine silver OR cotton thread for button and monogram detail
stuffing material
needles, pair, 3 1/4 mm (No. 10) and 4mm (No. 8)
sewing needle, long-eyed, suitable for yarn*

OPTIONAL (IF METHOD IS SIMPLIFIED):
*fabric paints (for mouth, nostrils, waistcoat detail, monogram, buttons)
tailor's chalk OR disappearing fabric marker
lentils (as a weight)
old nylon stocking (to hold lentils)*

MAIN TENSION
Measured over a 5cm (2in) square knitted plain.
14sts and 19 rows with 4ply yarn and 3 1/4 mm (No.10) knitting needles, or 10sts and 15 rows with DK yarn on 4mm (No.8) needles.

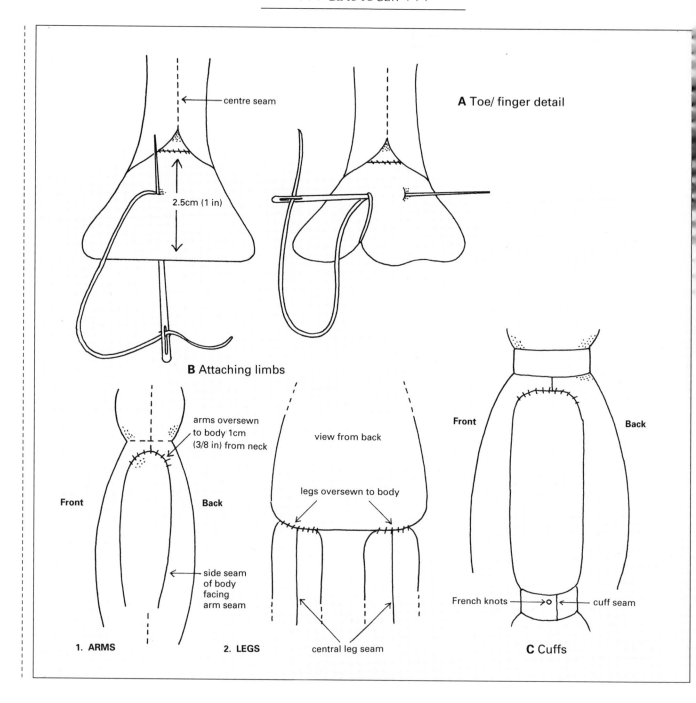

A Toe/ finger detail

centre seam

2.5cm (1 in)

B Attaching limbs

arms oversewn to body 1cm (3/8 in) from neck

Front

Back

side seam of body facing arm seam

1. ARMS

view from back

legs oversewn to body

2. LEGS

central leg seam

Front

Back

French knots

cuff seam

C Cuffs

METHOD

FROG

NOTE Use 3 1/4 mm, No.10, needles throughout.)

Head and Body (made as one piece):
Cast on 19sts with yarn B and st.st 2 rows. Join yarn C.
Work in Fair Isle pattern as follows, K odd rows and P even rows.
1st row: 2B,*1C, 3B, rep from * to end.
2nd row: 1B, *1C, 3B, rep from * ending with 1B.
3rd row: *1C, 3B, rep from * ending with 2B.
4th row: *3B, 1C, rep from * to end.
5th row: 2B, *1C, 3B, rep from * to end.
6th row: *3B, 1C, rep from * to end.
7th row: *1C, 3B, rep from * ending with 2B.
8th row: 1B, *1C, 3B, rep from * ending with 1B.
9th row: 2B, *1C, 3B, rep from * to end.
10th row: *3B, 1C, rep from * to end.
Repeat these ten pattern rows until work measures 19.5cm (7 3/4 in) from beginning. Change to following st.st pattern:
1st row: *1B, 1C, repeat from * to end.
2nd row: *1C, 1B, repeat from * to end.
Repeat these two pattern rows until work measures 30.5cm (12in)

from beginning. Break yarn C and st.st 2 rows plain. Cast off.

Arms (make 2 same):
Cast on 15sts with B and st.st 13cm (5 1/4 in). Cast off.

Legs (make 2 same):
Cast on 15sts with B and st.st 21cm (8 1/4 in). Cast off.

Bean Bag
Cast on 72sts with A and 4mm (No.8) needles.
St.st 35cm (13 3/4 in). Cast off.

HOW TO MAKE MR KROAK

● *NOTE Read the following notes before you begin*

1. Cast-on and cast-off edges of fabric are referred to as fabric ends and row-end edges are referred to as fabric sides.
2. Use stocking stitch side (smooth side) of fabric as right side.
3. Leave 1cm (3/8 in) seam allowances unless otherwise stated.
4. When stitching seams, work small back stitches in toning yarn.
5. When attaching eyes, make sure they are correctly positioned, as once washers have been pushed onto eye stems, they cannot be removed. To push washer onto stem, place pad of one thumb onto front of eye and push washer into place with fingers of both hands from reverse side of fabric. Take

care not to dig fingernail into casing, which should buckle with the pressure, as this will leave a mark.
6. When working features, secure thread as follows:
Knot end of thread and take needle into fabric and out at position of first stitch. Pull thread tight so that knot disappears beneath fabric and is caught in stuffing. Work a tiny stitch in same position to secure. To fasten off thread, take needle in and out of stuffing several times without catching fabric in stitches. Pull thread tight and cut close to fabric so that end disappears beneath fabric.
7. Make sure that all pieces are securely sewn in place if completed item is to be given to a young child.

Body: Fold body fabric in half, fabric ends and right sides together. Sew two long sides leaving 0.5cm (1/4 in) seam allowance. Turn to right side.

Eyes: Attach eyes to either side of head 1cm (3/8 in) from top fold and 1cm (3/8 in) from side seam, as described in Note 5 above.

Neck: Using double yarn, work a line of running stitches around body, 5.5cm (2 1/4 in) from top fold of body, starting and ending on same side seam. Do not fasten off. Stuff body. Pull ends of thread to gather fabric and form neck and fasten off.

Complete body: Tuck in remaining fabric edges at body base and oversew together.

Arms and legs (all limbs made the same way): Turn under edge on one short end of limb fabric, 0.5cm (1/4 in) to reverse side (purl side). (Make sure this is same edge on all limbs, i.e., weave of fabric runs in same direction.) Turn under same end again by 2.5cm (1in) and sew hem in place. This will become hand/foot of limb. Turn under edge on other short end to reverse side, once only by 0.5cm (1/4 in) and sew in place. Roll under two long sides to form a sausage shape with right side of fabric outermost. Oversew rolled edges together to form a central seam, beginning at hem line of hand/foot end. Oversew edges together at body end of limb.

Toes and fingers (same for all limbs): Using double yarn and holding limb with seam upper-most, work two evenly spaced double-stitches around toe/finger end of limb, 2cm (3/4 in) from end of limb and approximately 1.5cm (5/8 in) apart. Pull stitches tight to draw up fabric and create three toes/fingers. (See diagram A.)

Attaching arms to body: Oversew tops of shortest limbs to body with arm seams and side seams together and tops of arms 0.5cm (1/4 in) below neck. (See diagram B.)

Attaching legs: Oversew tops of remaining limbs to bottom seam of body with leg seams at centre back. (See diagram B.)

Mouth and nose: Embroider mouth, working a semi-circle of stem stitch with a single-length of red yarn and another semi-circle immediately below, with double body-green yarn. Work two French knots 1cm (3/8 in) apart above mouth for nostrils with a single-length of dark green yarn.

Collar and bow-tie: Cut a length of ribbon sufficient to wrap around neck with a 1.25cm (1/2 in) overlap. Press under ends of ribbon 0.5cm (1/4 in). Wrap ribbon around neck and sew folded edges to centre front of neck with cotton thread. Sew bow to collar seam.

Cuffs (both same): Make cuff as for collar, so that cuff seam is on outside back of arm. Embroider button using a single strand of black yarn or thread and working a French knot close to cuff seam. Complete button by working another French knot on top of black French knot using silver or cotton thread. (See diagram C.)

Waistcoat: Embroider points of waistcoat using a single-length of black yarn or thread and working stem stitch.

Embroider buttons as for cuffs and the letter 'K' with large straight stitches with single black yarn or thread. Then outline with straight stitches in silver or cotton thread.

Bean-bag: Fold bean-bag fabric in half, fabric sides and right sides together. Sew seam opposite fold. Turn to right side. Using double yarn, work a row of double stitches 1.25cm (1/2 in) from one edge. Pull thread to gather fabric tightly, pushing fabric edges to inside. Work a few stitches across centre of gathers to close hole. Work another row of running stitches 1.25cm (1/2 in) from other edge. Pull slightly. Stuff bean-bag very lightly until just under half full. Alternatively, if you are making the ornament to sit on a shelf, then fill a double-length of nylon stocking with a small amount of lentils. Make sure open ends of stocking are knotted securely, then insert into base of bean-bag beneath stuffing. Finish underside of bean-bag as for top. Push unstuffed end of bean-bag to inside and mould stuffing to form a bean-bag shape.

Opposite: Oxfam Globe Balls, Mr Kroak the Frog, Children round the World

Finally, sit Mr Kroak in his bean-bag with legs crossed and his arms resting on top of bean-bag.

Other ideas:

1. To simplify the knitting, omit Fair Isle patterning. Instead, work chest patterning in mint green and remainder in bright green.

OR

Substitute either block of patterning for stripes of two rows in each colour. This reduces the making time to approximately 6 hours.

2. To simplify the final decoration, use fabric paints for mouth, nostrils, waistcoat detail, monogram and buttons. First, draw out the lines with tailor's chalk or a disappearing fabric marker. Then apply the paint, following the manufacturer's instructions. Allow one colour to dry before applying another either on top or adjacent. This reduces the making time to approximately 5 hours.

3. Personalise your gift by substituting the monogram with the initials of the recipient. Alternatively, create your own Fair Isle pattern and use more than two colours.

4. Goo-goo eyes and ribbon bows can be purchased from craft shops or mail-order suppliers, addresses of which can be found in craft magazines. You can substitute the ribbon bow with a piece of narrow ribbon, either tied or stitched into a bow.

Mr Kroak takes about 8 hours to complete. If he is knitted from oddments and stuffed with washed nylon stockings, he can be made at almost no cost.

CHILDREN ROUND THE WORLD

These delightful miniature knitted dolls were designed especially for this book. When Jane Platt hears the word 'Oxfam' she thinks first of the children around the world who are fed and clothed by this charity. Oxfam's own quotation sums it up: Oxfam's support is given irrespective of race, colour, gender, politics or religion.

The Maker

Jane Platt has always enjoyed creative hobbies, learning to knit at age five. She later learned dressmaking, crochet, embroidery, tapestry, still-life painting and drawing, and began making her own creations.

Her career was in the computer industry when she married and had children. Juggling work and childcare arrangements became increasingly difficult, partly due to the inflexibility of employers toward working mothers. So, she turned her hobby into a business with more suitable working hours. She designs and sells decorative toys and ornaments by mail order, including hand and machine knitting patterns, plus knitted-up, ready-to-sew packs.

Jane Platt's ideas are inspired by the colours, shapes and patterns of nature. She aims to keep knitted pieces simple, many are rectangular. The final decorative effect is created by using contrasting yarns, worked together, embroidery, fancy edgings and attention to detail.

She is a member of the Knitting and Crochet Guild, and has contributed to *Woman's Weekly*, *Machine Knitting Monthly* and *Popular Crafts Magazine*.

The doll boys and girls come from Europe, Asia, Africa and South America. Their clothes suggest traditional dress.

Each doll is knitted quickly and simply, with the hair, head and body knitted as one rectangle. The arms and legs, also rectangular, are sewn on separately. The clothes are made with the simplest of shaping.

Step-by-step instructions

● **NOTE** *Size of completed doll: 10cm (4in)*

MATERIALS:
oddments of 4ply yarn
tiny amount of stuffing material (Use washed nylon stockings, cut very small OR waste yarn ends OR toy filling.)
pair 2 3/4 mm (No.12) knitting needles
long-eyed sewing needle, for yarn
yarn, cotton or embroidery thread (for face detail)

TENSION:
Tension square not necessary

How to make the dolls

Abbreviations and knitting instructions : See NOTES given for Mr Kroak.

Body

Cast on 16sts with knicker colour and st.st 8 rows

Change to vest colour (waistline) and st.st 8 rows
Change to face colour (neckline) and st.st 8 rows
Change to hair colour (top of head) and work according to hair style selected as follows:
Short straight hair - st.st 8 rows and cast off.
Short wavy hair - g.st 8 rows and cast off
Short curly hair - K 1 row, rev.st.st 7 rows beg with K row. Cast off.
Long wavy hair - st.st 8 rows, g.st 9 rows and cast off.
Very long straight hair - st.st 24 rows and cast off.

To make up body:

Fold body in half lengthways, right sides tog and matching colour changes. Sew long seam with matching yarn. With seam at centre back, oversew base of body. Turn to right side. Stuff body to waistline. Work a line of small running sts along last row of knickers. Pull to shape waist and fasten off. Rep process stuffing chest and gathering last row to shape neck. Finally stuff head and gather last row of face tightly to close gap. Leave hair seam open.

Hair:

Neaten cast-off thread at hair end. Leaving sides of hair curled under, fold hair down to cover back of head and catch in place at sides of face and base of neck. Work two long sts of yarn across

top of head to make a head-band or bind long hair to make a ribbon or hair-band.

Features:

Do not set features too far down on face otherwise the mouth will be hidden by the clothing. Work each eye with three small sts close together and a tiny st at centre for pupil. Work eyebrows and mouth with a single st. Work nose and ears with several sts on top of each other in face colour. For earrings, work a French knot for studs or a tiny loop for hoops at the base of each ear.

Arms (make 2 same):

Cast on 6sts wih skin colour and st.st 10 rows.
Break yarn leaving a long end for sewing and thread through rem sts. Pull yarn tight to form end of hand and oversew sides together, right side outside. Stuff using a knitting needle point or a closed pair of small pointed scissors. Sew open end to side of body just below neckline with seam underneath. To make a bracelet, secure a length of yarn at position of bracelet. (See NOTES for Mr Kroak.) Wrap yarn twice around arm and fasten off.

Legs (make 2 same):

Cast on 6sts with skin colour.
To make bare legs and feet:
St.st 14 rows. Break yarn and thread through sts. Make as for

arms and sew to either side of body base with seams at the back.

To make socks and shoes:
St.st 7 rows in skin colour. Change to sock colour. P 2 rows and K 1 row. Change to shoe colour. St.st 4 rows. Break yarn and thread through sts. Complete as above, sewing shoe seam with end thread and rem of leg with skin-coloured yarn. For lace-up shoes, embroider three small sts across front of shoe, knotting and trimming yarn ends at top of shoe.

To make sandals or shoes without socks:
St.st 10 rows in skin colour and 4 rows in sandal colour. Make up as above. For sandals, embroider sts with skin colour across front of foot to represent skin showing between sandal straps.

Clothes

● *NOTE The colours are given against each item of clothing to enable you to easily identify the garment in the picture.*

Jumper (make front and back the same): (random-coloured)
Cast on 24sts. Continue in st.st and work 6 rows.
Cast off 6sts at beg of next two rows to shape arms.
St.st 6 rows.
P 1 row and cast off K-wise.
To make. Join jumper pieces tog at sides and undersides of sleeves. Place on doll. Join shoulders and top of sleeves.

Variations. Use random-coloured yarn or knit stripes as follows:
Cast on with A. Continue in 2 row stripes of A and B, beg with B.
For a Fair Isle effect, sew up jumper and reverse side outside or knit striped jumper entirely in g.st.

● *NOTE For the doll dressed in the short gathered skirt and Fair Isle effect jumper, the skirt has been wrapped over the jumper hem.*

Boy's long tunic (make front and back the same): (pale-blue)
Cast on 24sts. Continue in st.st and work 6 rows.
Cast off 6sts at beg of next two rows to shape sleeves. St.st 14 rows, increasing at each end of first and seventh of these rows.
Decrease at each end of next row.
Cast off but P 2 tog at either end of row.
To make. Make as for jumper but leave lower 1.5cm (1/2 in) of side seam open. Embroider buttons down front with French knots.

T-shirt (make front and back the same): (yellow-and-blue stripes)
Cast on 16sts with A. Join B and work in 2 row stripes throughout beg with B as follows:
St.st 6 rows. Cast off 2sts at beg of next 2 rows to shape sleeves.
St.st 6 rows. P 1 row and cast off K-wise.
To make. Make as for jumper.

Girl's blouse (front and back the same): (lilac with pink trim)

Cast on 14sts with main and st.st 6 rows. Cast off 2sts at beg of next 2 rows. St.st 4 rows. Fasten off main and join contrast. P 1 row and cast-off K-wise.
To make. Make as for jumper.

Sleeveless top (make front and back the same): (red)
Cast on 14sts and st.st 8 rows.
P 1 row and cast off K-wise for hem.
To make. Join sides. Place on doll and join shoulders.

Short straight skirt (one piece): (denim blue)
Cast on 18sts and K 2 rows for hem. St.st 9 rows beg with P row. (K2tog, K1) to end of row -12sts.
Cast off.
To make. Wrap around doll's waist and join the sides with the seam at the back.

Long gathered skirt (one piece): (lilac with pink trim)
Cast on 56sts with contrast. Change to main and K 1 row.
St.st 14 rows beg with K row. (K2tog) to end of row to shape waist -28sts.
(P2tog) to end of row -14sts.
Cast off.
To make. Wrap around doll's waist and join sides with seam at back.

Short gathered skirt (one piece): (brown with red trim)
Cast on 28sts with contrast and K 1 row.

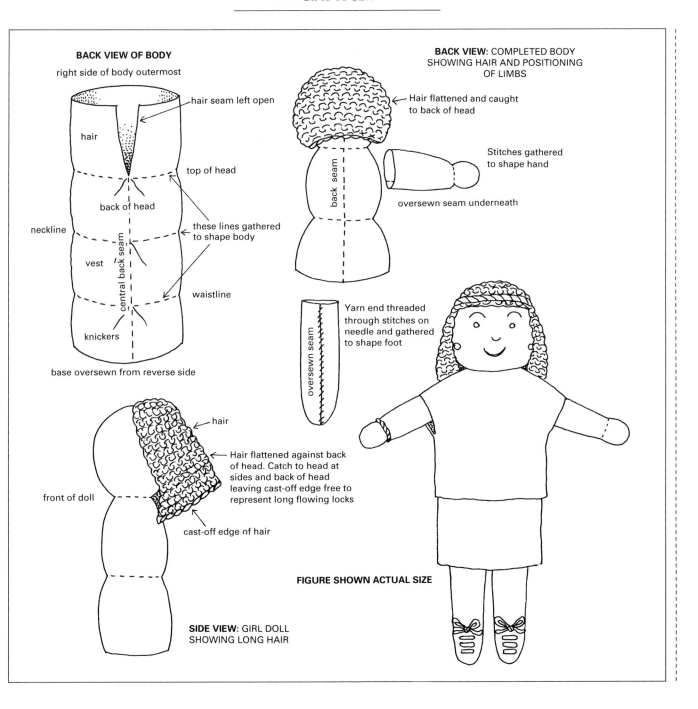

BACK VIEW OF BODY

right side of body outermost

hair seam left open

hair

top of head

back of head

these lines gathered to shape body

neckline

vest

central back seam

waistline

knickers

base oversewn from reverse side

BACK VIEW: COMPLETED BODY SHOWING HAIR AND POSITIONING OF LIMBS

Hair flattened and caught to back of head

Stitches gathered to shape hand

back seam

oversewn seam underneath

Yarn end threaded through stitches on needle and gathered to shape foot

oversewn seam

hair

Hair flattened against back of head. Catch to head at sides and back of head leaving cast-off edge free to represent long flowing locks

front of doll

cast-off edge of hair

SIDE VIEW: GIRL DOLL SHOWING LONG HAIR

FIGURE SHOWN ACTUAL SIZE

Join in main. St.st 2 rows. P 2 rows with contrast and fasten off contrast. St.st 10 rows main. (K2tog) to end of row to shape waist. Cast-off P-wise.
To make. As for long gathered skirt.

Sleeveless dress (make front and back the same): (deep pink with white trim)
Cast on 14sts with contrast for hem. Change to main. K 1 row.
St.st 16 rows beg with K row. Join in contrast and P2tog to end of row. K 1 row. Fasten off contrast. St.st 6 rows with main. Cast off.
To make. Join sides seam. Place on doll and catch top corners tog at shoulders.

Girl's bag: (deep pink)
Bag. Cast on 6sts and st.st 14 rows. Cast off.
Fold in half, right side outside and oversew sides.
Sew two long lengths of yarn between tops of side seams for handle, wrapping one around the other.

Hat: (one grey and one brown)
Cast on 30sts with main and st.st 3 rows. P2tog to end of row. Change to contrast and K 1 row.
Change back to main and st.st 3 rows beg with P row.
P 1 row. St.st 2 rows. Break yarn and thread through sts.
To make. Pull yarn end to gather sts tight and join sides of hat tog.

Stuff top of hat. With hat seam at back, sew hat to doll's head along base of hat band.

Straight trousers: (light or dark grey)
Cast on 9sts and st.st 13 rows ending with K row for one trouser leg.
Mark beg of last row and leave sts on needle.
Cast 9sts onto other needle for other trouser leg. St.st 13 rows and mark end of last row.
St.st 11 rows across all 18sts on needle beg with a P row, pulling yarn end tight at beg of second leg. Cast off leaving a long end for sewing.
To make. Join side seam down to markers with end thread. Then join side seams of each leg tog. Place on doll with the seam at the back.

Baggy trousers: (pale blue)
Cast on 7sts and st.st 2 rows for leg hem. Inc in every st of next row 14sts. St.st 12 rows beg with P row. Mark beg of this row. Break yarn and leave.
Cast 7sts onto another needle and make another leg. Mark end of last row.
St.st 9 rows across all 28sts beg with a P row, pulling yarn end tight at beg of second leg. (K2tog) to end of row and cast off P-wise.
To make. Make up as for straight trousers but place on doll before sewing back seam.

Shorts: (beige)
Cast on 14sts and K 2 rows for one leg. Break yarn and leave.
Cast another 14sts onto same needle and rep for other leg.
Then P across all sts completing as given for Baggy trousers.
To make. Wrap around doll's waist and join back seam. Sew leg seams tog.

✳ *HINTS: To reduce the making time, paint on the faces with fabric paints using a fine paint brush, following manufacturer's ins-tructions.*

Each doll will take about two hours to make. They can be adapted to make a variety of gifts, as lovely additions for a child's doll house, or sewn onto a jumper or cardigan for an original three-dimensional effect. If a length of narrow cord or ribbon is sewn through the doll's head, they can be made into fun key-fobs, even necklaces. Or, sew a brooch fastening, available from craft suppliers, to the doll's back to make an unusual brooch.

TRAVELLER'S EMERGENCY KIT

by Jennie Smith for the Townswomen's Guilds

This pretty little handy-bag will carry those essentials we don't always know we need until we need them – needle, thread, little scissors, tissues, plaster, bandages, aspirin, and safety pins. The kit is ideal for the car, a suitcase or even a handbag. Vary the contents to suit the recipient, and the size of the bag to suit the contents. Contents variation for walkers: bar of chocolate, whistle (if you are going into the hills) and sheep's wool for tops of boots (there is always someone with new boots or walking shoes). Contents variation for someone going into hospital: comb, notelets, pen and pencil, small note pad, some stamps, money for papers, a little bottle of perfume.
How does the Traveller's Emergency Kit meet the Oxfam Anniversary theme? 'Waste not, want not.'

Step-by-step instructions

MATERIALS:
cotton or polycotton remnants
thin card scraps, all same weight (to make templates)
zip fastener OR *strip of velcro 15cm (6in) long*
drima cotton (for oversewing)
Contents for the kit: tissues, bandages, and so on (your choice)

METHOD
1. Plan the colours for your handy-bag. Then gather together your pieces of material. Use material with small patterns and contrasting colours.
2. Cut 18 templates 5cm (2in) square from scrap card.
3. Make a larger template 7.5cm (3in) square from card.
4. Press the fabric.
5. Take the 7.5cm (3in) square template, and cut 18 squares of fabric.
6. Tack the 18 squares of fabric to the 18 pieces of card 5cm (2in) square.
7. Placing the squares side by side, 6 deep and 3 wide, oversew them together by hand, two at a time, right sides together, just taking up the fabric, not the card.
8. When all the patches are oversewn together, take out tacking stitches and card and press.
9. Tack wadding or soft interlining to back of fabric
10. Then tack lining fabric to side that will be inside.
11. Hand-quilt or machine over-lock through 3 thicknesses on the seam lines.
12. Sew in zipper or velcro.
13. Sew up sides, making a bag.
14. Place the contents in the Traveller's Emergency Kit.

✱ *HINT The basic idea can be adapted to a bag any size, including a shopping bag.*

The kit is easy to make, and costs almost nothing. The work invested is repaid with a thoughtful handmade gift.

The Contributor
The Townswomen's Guilds (TG) are committed to advancing the social awareness of women irrespective of age, race, creed or political affiliation. There are more than 100,000 members throughout the UK who meet regularly to exchange ideas, learn new skills and take part in a wide range of activities. TG mounts a strong lobby on national and regional issues.

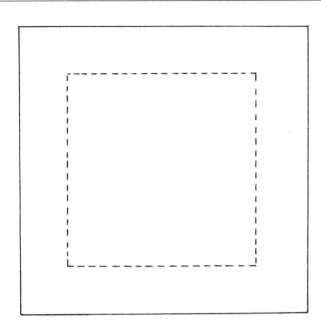

TEMPLATES

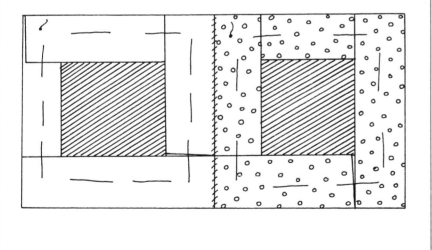

The Maker
Jennie Smith first learned to do patchwork and quilting during the war. Her interest was sparked by a beautiful counterpane in the window of a Red Cross Shop on the Isle of Man, where her husband was briefly posted. She walked past the shop every day, and still remembers the pale pink, green and blue hexagons of this bedcovering!

When she returned home, she began experimenting with all the odds and ends of plain and patterned cottons at her mother's home, for her mother was a dressmaker. Jennie's first template was made of plywood, which worked quite well. Unusually, she began with a quilt, and later made the simpler tea cosies and cushions. Soon her mother, sister, and sister-in-law joined in the patchwork and quilting. Then she joined the Embroiderer's Guild at Newcastle.

Now she teaches at Action in Retirement, Sunderland, makes displays for local exhibitions and shows, and is a member of the Townswomen's Guild.

OXFAM GLOBE BALL

by Althea Tyndale

The design of the Oxfam Globe Ball symbolises harmonious working together and different peoples. The ball has four coloured sections in the Oxfam Anniversary colours with contrasting strips over the seams and around the Equator and Tropics of Capricorn and of Cancer to form a globe. Bands of caring and sharing link the four quarters, stretching from east to west and from north to south.

Step-by-step instructions

● **NOTE** *Materials and method are for three balls – 1 large, 1 medium, 1 small.*

MATERIALS:

felt: Generally sold in pieces 30cm (12in) square. Buy different coloured 30cm (12in) squares in the Oxfam Anniversary colours. (Keep the leftover pieces; they may come in handy for a felt appliqué project.)
OR
cloth: 5 pieces, approx 23cm (¹/₄yd) in different colours. Use left-overs, sale bargains or (more expensively) new pieces in the Oxfam Anniversary colours. (This amount makes 4-8 small balls, depending on the width of fabric.)
stuffing: Use recycled material such as old nylons, or bits of otherwise unuseable clean cloth, rags, ends of thread, and so on.
thread: matching colour for the decorative strips. Any colour for the seams, as they will be covered.
strips: For the felt ball - Cut felt strips 1cm (³/₈ in) wide for a large ball,
proportionally narrower for smaller balls.
strips: For the cloth ball - either narrow ribbon about 0.5cm (¹/₄ in) wide OR bias-binding folded in two OR (for the more advanced) self-made bias-binding about 1 ¹/₂ in (³/₄ in) wide, folded in three to make a 0.5cm (¹/₄ in) strip.
Length needed for a small ball - 1.5m (5ft), proportionally more for larger balls.
pins: Preferably with coloured glass heads, so they won't disappear into the felt. (Count the pins before you begin, and check the number after you've finished.)

✳ *HINT When pinning strips onto the ball, always place pins in vertically to prevent stretching out of shape.*

METHOD
Making the template:
1. Take a piece of paper (any sort), the width being a little more than half the length. (If the width is exactly half the length, the result will be a square ball, and not a proper globe.) Fold in four. Place as in diagram.
2. With wrist on table, draw a curve by sweeping pen or pencil from base to top, left to right (reverse paper and reverse direction if you are left-handed).
3. Keeping paper folded, cut along the curve. Unfold and smooth out. Trim, if necessary.
4. Place on a piece of thin card (eg. back of writing pad/cereal packet) and draw round the outline carefully. Cut out carefully. This is your template.

✳ *HINT Make several templates first, to check whether you have made the size you want. If you are uncertain, make four of the same size and pin them together down the edges to make a trial ball. When you are sure, take the template you like best and transfer it to the card.*

Cutting the material:
Place template on material, hold down firmly and draw round it. Allowing 1cm (¹/₂ in) seam allowance, cut four quarters.

Felt – Has no grain, and can be cut in whatever direction is most convenient and economical. Try not to pull it about, as it stretches out of shape easily.
Cloth – Cut on straight grain.

❋ *HINT Felt makes a rounder ball than cloth does.*

Sewing order:

1. Sew three seams and about two-thirds of the way up the fourth seam.

(If you are advanced enough, temporarily finish off this incomplete seam with a double-stitch, and pull the thread through to the right side, so you have enough thread left to close the seam after you've stuffed the ball. This prevents puckering.)

2. Clip the edges, including the unsewn bit of the uncompleted seam.

3. Turn.

4 Stuff ball as hard or soft as you like.

● **NOTE** *Don't over-stuff the large ball, as it will be rather heavy and uncomfortable for a small child.*

Remember, the harder you stuff the ball, the heavier it is and the more it will cost to post.

5. Sew the remaining bit of seam, preferably with a running stitch along the seam line. This 'pulls' less than an overstitched seam, and lies flatter.

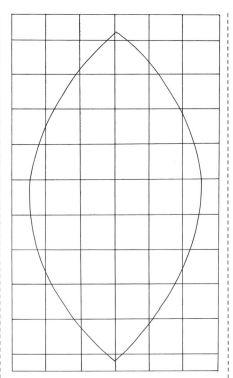

Above: *To save time, here is a scaled template for the Oxfam Globe Ball. Each square = 2.5cm (1in).*

Sewing on the decorative strips:

1. Find the Equator by stretching a tape measure from Pole to Pole, and place a pin in vertically at the mid-point. Do this right round the ball. The measurements will vary slightly, being more along the seam-lines and less along the middle of each quarter.

2. Lay a strip carefully around the Equator, without pulling it at all, and pin in place, with the ends meeting on any one of the longitudinal seams.

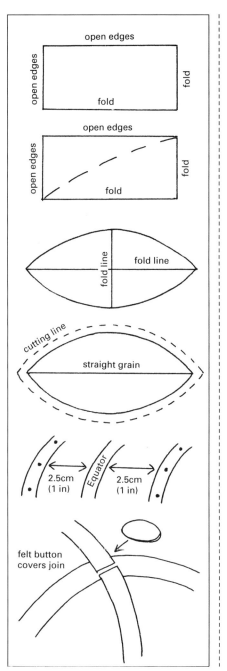

3. Stitch down neatly along both edges.

4. Place pins along Tropics.

Small ball – 2.5cm (1in) from edge of Equator strip to centre of Tropic strip.

Medium ball – 3.75cm (1 1/2 in)

Large ball – 5cm (2in)

Pin strips along Tropics, and sew neatly down both edges.

5. Place the longitudinal strips over the long seams, with the edges at the Poles. Tuck the ends under the strip above, as in diagram, so that all joins are now hidden.

● *NOTE As the felt squares may not be large enough to provide a complete length to encircle the globe, you may have to cut strips of shorter length. The Equator and Tropic ends will be hidden by the longitudinal strips, but you may end up with a visible join at the Poles. The Poles can be covered with a small felt 'button', as shown in diagram.*

To make button: Draw round a coin of suitable size, or the bottom of a reel of thread. Cut out very carefully, pin in place and sew neatly all round.

● *NOTE **Don't** use a real button. This is dangerous. It can hurt when thrown, and can be chewed off and swallowed by a baby or pet.*

The Maker
My mother taught me to sew when I was about four years old, and I've rarely been without some needlework project on the go since then. My favourite is patchwork quilting, which I've been doing for years and years, now semi-professionally. Some of my craft work is sold through a crafts gallery, some privately and some given away as gifts.

I taught needlework briefly at a girls' boarding schol, but prefer to keep the sewing as a paying hobby, rather than a full-time career.

Approximate sewing time:
Hand-sewing – upwards of five hours. Felt is much quicker and easier to sew than cloth.
Machine-sewing – Obviously much quicker, but unless you possess a very advanced machine, you'll still have to finish the ball by hand.

● *NOTE Felt: Not washable; it shrinks. Dry clean.*
Cloth: Washable, drip or tumble dry. Don't iron; the polyester or nylon stuffing will melt.

The Oxfam Globe Ball can be the basis for other balls in cloth or felt, for all occasions. By your choice of fabrics and decoration, you can make personalised birthday party balls, or ones for an anniversary or Christmas.

Opposite: Soft Animals, Child's Rag Book

SOFT ANIMALS

by Jessica and Jenny Bryne-Daniel for Designers of Distinction

Here is a stable full of ponies, unicorns and donkeys – and accessories.
Part of the fun will be finding fabrics and scraps in colours, textures and weights that are 'just right' for a certain creature.
A soft toy is relatively easy to make, and gives comfort and pleasure.
The patterns can be adapted to make even more animals, such as zebras (using stripy material or embroidered stripes), circus horses (spotted and decorated), Welsh mountain ponies and mules.

PONY, UNICORN AND DONKEY

Step-by-step instructions

MATERIALS:
felt OR *closely woven woollen fabric,*
  50 x 30cm (1 ¹/₂ x 1ft)
Pony: scraps of woollen yarn for mane and tail
Unicorn: scraps of woollen yarn and thread for mane and tail. Gilt tag end OR *golden fabric and stiff canvas for horn.*
Donkey: scraps of pale, hairy fabric for inner ears and tummy
stuffing: sheep's wool, Kapok OR *finely chopped old nylons*
cotton (for sewing)
felt, black (for eyes)
fabric adhesive
fray check
scissors
OPTIONAL:
plastic OR *leather thonging for harness*
sequins and beads for harness, eyes or decoration

METHOD
1. Place and pin the pattern pieces on the cloth. Fit them together carefully to avoid wasting fabric. Cut out pattern pieces.
2. Match one of the side pieces (A) to one of the tummy gussets (B). Stab stitch (small, firm, strong stitch) from the chest down the leg (leave foot open), up the front leg, along the tummy, down the hind leg (leave foot open) and up hind leg to top of gusset. Repeat with the other side piece and tummy gusset.
3. Put the 2 side pieces together with the tummy gussets inside. Neatly stab stitch along the back and under the head, leaving the top of the head open for the face gusset.
4. Stab stitch half of face gusset. For Pony, in white, if blaze is required.
5. Firmly stuff head and sew up other side of face gusset.
6. Firmly stuff legs and sew on hoof gussets.

7. Firmly stuff neck and body. Sew together tummy gusset, pulling the two sides together as firmly as possible.
8. *To make tail:* Wind long lengths of yarn around hand. Sew on. Cut loop ends.
9. *To make ears:* Fold together ears at base and sew on ear pieces.
10. *To make mane:* Take 2 long lengths of thick woollen yarn, and sew with ordinary sewing thread.
   Form a bundle of yarn by winding the wool around a pencil or your finger, and sew between the ears so that the wool falls over the face as the forelock. Snip loop ends for fringe.
   Now work down the upper neck line, forming loops of yarn by winding it 3 times around a pencil.
   Stitch the group of loops onto the neck through the bottom of the loops.
   Lightly overlap each group of loops.
11. *Eyes:* Stick on black felt eyes.

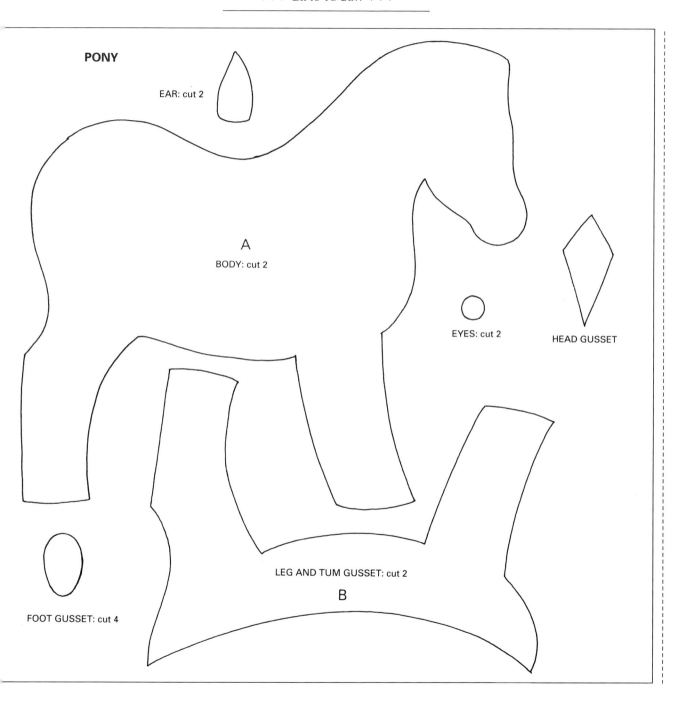

PONY

EAR: cut 2

A

BODY: cut 2

EYES: cut 2

HEAD GUSSET

FOOT GUSSET: cut 4

LEG AND TUM GUSSET: cut 2

B

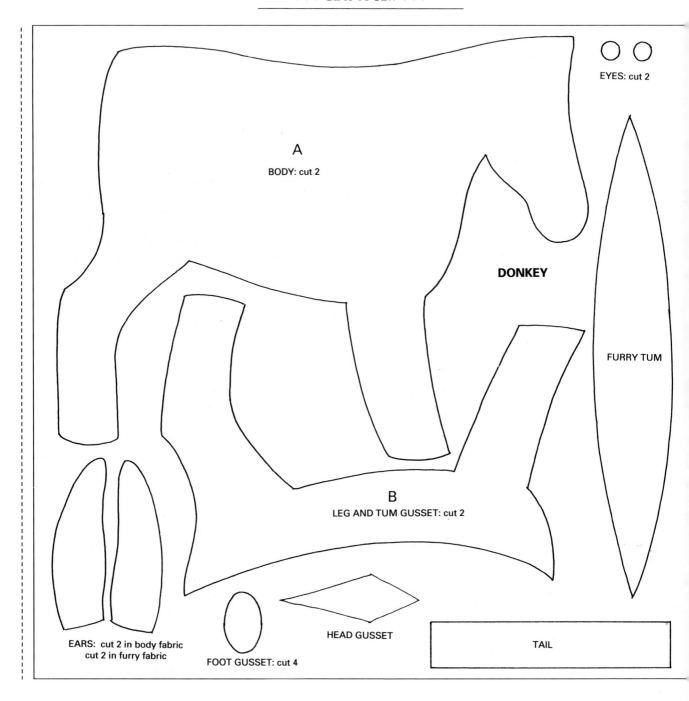

EYES: cut 2

A

BODY: cut 2

DONKEY

FURRY TUM

B

LEG AND TUM GUSSET: cut 2

EARS: cut 2 in body fabric
cut 2 in furry fabric

FOOT GUSSET: cut 4

HEAD GUSSET

TAIL

Unicorn variations

1. Add some shimmering threads to mane and tail.

2. *For tail:* Cut a narrow length of felt stitched in half with a bundle of loops, like the forelock, inserted in the end and stitched in.

3. *For the horn:* Sew on a gilt tag end OR a cone of canvas covered with golden fabric. Secure with adhesive or sew between the ears.

Donkey variations

1. Use adapted pattern, and proceed as for Pony.

2. Cut the mane loops.

3. Line the ears with hairy fabric, and stitch on a hairy tummy.

✳ *HINT Decorate your soft toy with sequins and beads.*

Tack for pony and donkey

1. For bridle and head collar, make from leather thonging OR plastic, and link rings for bit rings.

2. For rugs, make from woollen fabric OR knit. Fasten at chest with ribbons, hook and eye OR button and loop. The rug can be personalised by embroidering the owner's initials in the rear corner.

These patterns can be adapted to make other animals. Use the donkey pattern, and striped material to make a zebra.

The Makers

Jessica and Jenny Bryne-Daniel run a design practice in Wales. Their original designs often highlight embroidery and other textile techniques. They teach and have written about crafts.

They believe that anything that focuses on animals helps in some way to promote the care and understanding of animals.

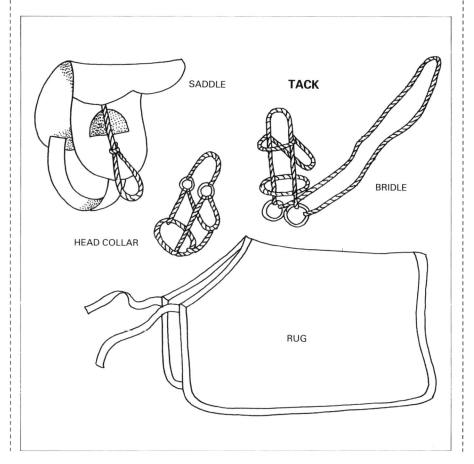

SADDLE

TACK

HEAD COLLAR

BRIDLE

RUG

KILIM JACKET

by Kaffe Fassett

The inspiration for the pattern on this beautiful jacket was the design on a kilim carpet. Kilims are traditional prayer mats and are made throughout the Middle East. Kilim carpets from the Azara people of Central Afghanistan sometimes feature in the Oxfam catalogue. These carpets are made by refugees in Pakistan with support and training from the Ockenden Venture, a national charity that works with refugees around the world. Two very different worlds converge here in Kaffe Fassett's Kilim Jacket.

Step-by-step instructions

ABBREVIATIONS:

K	knit
P	purl
st(s)	stitch(es)
inc	increas(ing)
dec	decreas(ing)
st st	stocking stitch
beg	begin(ning)
foll	following
rep	repeat
alt	alternate
cont	continue
patt	pattern
tog	together
mm	millimetres
cm	centimetres
in	inch(es)
RS	right side
WS	wrong side
M1	make 1

MATERIALS: YARN
Rowan Kid Silk, Rowanspun Tweed, Light Tweed, Silk Stones, Light Weight D.K., Fox Tweed D.K., Thick Cotton Chenile, Fine Cotton Chenile, Donegal Lambswool Tweed, Wool/Cotton and Botany.

See yarn chart opposite
The finer yarns are used in combination, e.g., SS – use two strands of yarn S, Za – use one strand of yarn Z and one yarn a.

For the combinations of yarns denoted by symbols on the chart, refer to the chart key.

NEEDLES:
1 pair 5mm (No.6)
1 pair 6mm (No.4)

BUTTONS:
5

TENSION:
15st and 20 rows to 10cm (4in) measured over patt st st using 6mm (No.4) needles.

METHOD
Back
Cast on 92sts using 5mm (No.6) needles and yarn FR.
Work 17 rows in K1, P1 rib in the foll colour sequence.
2 rows GF, 2 rows GMd, 2 rows jjhmn (symbol X), 2 rows JPB, 1 row BT, 3 rows Cd, 1 row Oq, 1 row Fe, 2 rows fG, 1 row Re.
Next Row WS (inc): Using yarn Re, rib 4 (M1, rib 3) 29 times, rib (121 sts).
Change to 6mm (No.4) needle and joining in and breaking of colours as required, cont in pat from chart for back. Use separate lengths of yarn for each area o contrast colour. Link one colour to the next by twisting them around each other where they meet on the WS to avoid gaps.
Work 120 rows in patt, marking each end of rows 12 and 46 for pocket openings, ending with a WS row.

Divide for Neck
Patt 52 sts turn and leave rem sts on a holder.
Work each side of neck separately
Cast off 4 sts beg next row, patt to end.
Cast off rem sts.
With RS facing rejoin yarns to rem sts, cast off centre 17 sts. patt to end.

		Shade no.	Amount				Shade no	Amount
A	Kid Silk Turnip	997	1 x 25gm (1oz)		U	Fox Tweed Cricket	851	1 x 50gm (2oz)
B	Kid Silk Old Gold	989	2 x 25gm (1oz)		V	Kid Silk Potpourri	996	2 x 25gm (1oz)
C	Kid Silk Smoke	998	2 x 25gm (1oz)		W	Don.Lbs.Twd.Rye	474	1 x 25gm (1oz)
D	Kid Silk Silver Blonde	995	2 x 25gm (1oz)		Y	Lt.Wt.DK.	54	1 x 25gm (1oz)
E	Rowanspun Caper	762	1 x 100gm (4oz)		Z	Don.Lbs.Twd.Pepper	473	2 x 25gm (1oz)
F	Rowanspun Caviar	760	2 x 100gm (4oz)		a	Fox Tweed Seal	852	1 x 50gm (2oz)
G	Lt.Tweed Rosemix	215	3 x 25gm (1oz)		b	Lt.Wt.DK.	624	2 x 25gm (1oz)
H	Lt.Tweed Bracken	204	2 x 25gm (1oz)		d	Don.Lbs.Twd.Bark	475	3 x 25gm (1oz)
J	Lt.Tweed Bamboo	218	2 x 25gm (1oz)		e	Don.Lbs.Twd.Elderberry	490	2 x 25gm (1oz)
K	Lt.Tweed Dragonfly	228	1 x 25gm (1oz)		f	Rowanspun Fig	761	1 x 100gm (4oz)
L	Lt.Tweed Charcoal	210	4 x 25gm (1oz)		g	Kid Silk Garnet	992	1 x 25gm (1oz)
M	Silk Stones Blue Mist	832	1 x 50gm (2oz)		h	Wool/Cotton Kashmir	910	2 x 40gm (1 1/2 oz)
N	Silk Stones Marble	833	1 x 50gm (2oz)		j	Lt.Tweed Garnet	226	3 x 25gm (1oz)
O	Silk Stones Eau de nil	835	1 x 50gm (2oz)		m	Lt.Tweed Hydrangea	229	2 x 25gm (1oz)
P	Lt.Wt.DK.	86	3 x 25gm (1oz)		n	Botany	118	2 x 25gm (1oz)
q	Lt.Wt.DK.	605	3 x 25gm (1oz)		r	Thick Chen.Wild Cherry	370	1 x 100gm (4oz)
R	Lt.Wt.DK.	65	3 x 25gm (1oz)		t	Don.Lbs.Twd.Taragon	477	1 x 25gm (1oz)
S	Lt.Wt.DK.	61	3 x 25gm (1oz)		y	Fox Tweed Wren	850	2 x 50gm (2oz)
T	Lt.Wt.DK.	412	2 x 25gm (1oz)					

KEY

r		HV	
hjjmn		ag	
fL		LLS	
MN		Td	
RV		bdd	
LR		JJN	
LLL		ad	
JJP		GV	
Kq		Dg	
BH		Hq	
PP		NN	
FL		RR	
SS		Nf	
Ra		Nq	
Re		FY	
LSe		yZ	

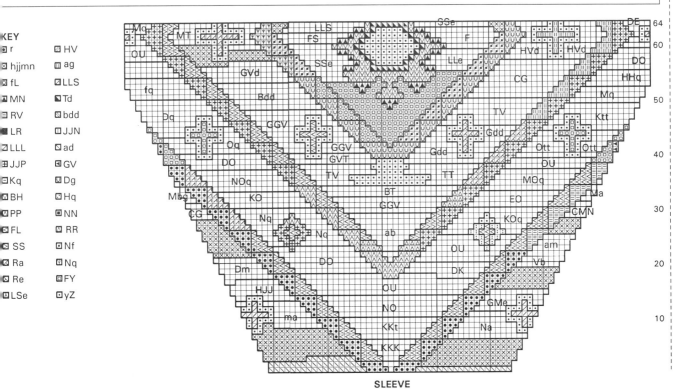

SLEEVE

87

Work 1 row.
Complete to match first side reversing all shaping and foll chart for left back.

Left front

Cast on 46 sts using 5mm (No.6) needles and yarn FR.
Work 17 rows in K1, P1, rib as given for back.
Next Row (inc): Using yarns Re rib 3 (M1, rib 3) 14 times, rib 1. (60 sts)
Change to 6mm (No.4) needles and joining in and breaking off colours as given for back, work 75 rows in patt from chart for left front, marking positions of pocket opening on side edge as for back.

Shape front neck

Next Row WS: Cast off 3 sts patt to end.
Work 3 rows without shaping.
Dec 1 st at beg next row and every foll 4th row until 48 sts remain.
Continue without any further shaping until front matches back to shoulder ending with a WS row.

Shape shoulder

Cast off.

Right front

Work as given for left front reversing all shaping and foll chart for right front.

Sleeves (both alike)

Cast on 31 sts using 5mm (No.6) needles and yarns FR. Work 17

rows in K1, P1 rib as given for back.
Next Row (inc): Using yarns Re, rib 3 (M1, rib 2) 14 times. (45 sts)
Change to 6mm (No.4) needles and joining in and breaking off colours as given for back, work 64 rows in patt from chart for sleeve and AT THE SAME TIME shape sides by inc 1 st each end of 3rd row and every foll alt row until there are 97 sts. Take extra sts into patt as they occur.
Cast off loosely and evenly.

Making up

Use backstitch for all main knitting seams and an edge to edge stitch for all ribs unless stated otherwise.
Press all pieces (except ribbing) on WS using a warm iron over a damp cloth.
Join both shoulder seams.
Pocket edgings (both alike)
With RS facing 5mm (No.6) needles and yarn f pick up and knit 30 sts evenly betwen markers on side edge of front.
K1 row to form hemline.
Work a further 4 rows in st st beg with a knit row.
Cast off loosely and evenly.

Left pocket lining

With RS facing 6mm (No.4) needles and yarn f pick up and knit 31 sts evenly between markers on left side edge of back and cont in st st beg with a purl row and AT THE SAME TIME cast on 8

sts at beg of first row and dec 1 st at end of 5th row and every foll alt row until 24 sts remain.
Cast off evenly.

Right pocket lining

Work as given for left pocket lining reversing all shaping.

Buttonhole band

With RS facing, 5mm (No.6) needles and yarns FR pick up and knit 67 sts evenly along right front edge for a woman's jacket, left front edge for a man's.
Next row (buttonhole): P4 (cast off 2 sts, P13) 4 times, cast off 2 sts, P3.
Next row: Knit across row casting on 2 sts to replace those cast off on previous row.
Next row: Knit to form foldline.
Work a further 8 rows in st st beg with a knit row and work buttonholes on rows 2 and 3 to correspond with those made previously.
Cast off loosely and evenly.

Buttonband

Work as given for buttonhole band omitting buttonholes.

Collar

Cast on 133 sts using 5mm (No.6) needles and yarns FR.
Cont in K1, P1 rib in colour sequence outlined below and AT THE SAME TIME shape collar by casting off 4 sts at beg of 7th row and every foll row until 17 sts remain.

Colour sequence: 2 rows FG, 2 rows GMd, 2 rows jjmhn, 2 rows JPB, 1 row BT, 3 rows Cd, 1 row Oq, 1 row Fe, 2 rows fG, 3 rows LRe, 2 rows CRG, 3 rows jjmhn, 3 rows BOe, 2 rows FR, 1 row Wdd, 4 rows SeL, 2 rows GVd.
Cast off using GVd.

Fold front bands to WS along foldline and slip st loosely into place. Attach shaped edge of collar neatly to neckline, having centre back of cast off row to centre back neck and cast on edge of collar and foldlines of front bands in one continuous line.
Place markers 32cm (12in) down from shoulder seam on back and fronts.
Set in sleeve between markers
Join sleeve seams and side seams above and below pocket markers.
Fold pocket edgings to WS along foldline and slip st loosely in place.
Slip st pocket linings loosely to WS of jacket fronts.
Sew on buttons to correspond with buttonholes.
Press seams.

This magnificent gift will require an investment of time and money. The result will be a jacket that is a work of art.

The Maker
Kaffe Fassett is one of the world's most brilliant and inspiring designer-knitters. Influences as diverse as Turkoman carpets, Japanese ikat weaving, a tiled floor in Pompeii and a Spanish damask cloth have inspired his designs which are a magnificent blend of colour and pattern that transcends the fashion of the moment.

Opposite: Kilim Jacket

SILKEN WALL HANGING

by Bernadette Falvey for the Irish Countrywomen's Association

This beautiful wall hanging is entitled 'Hope'. The patchwork block 'Peace and Plenty' has been used as its basis. To Bernadette Falvey both titles are synonymous with 'It's Time for a Fairer World.'

Step-by-step instructions

● **NOTE** *The wall hanging is approximately 76cm (30in) square.*

MATERIALS:

● **NOTE** *Work out your colour scheme and choose your fabrics first. Fabric can be silk OR cotton OR scraps. The colours given here are those of the example in the photograph.*

1.4m (1 1/2yd) green fabric, 1.2m (48in) wide

30cm (1/3yd) blue fabric, 1.2m (48in) wide

23cm (1/4yd) white fabric, 1.2m (48in) wide

batting, 1 piece, 90 x 90cm (36 x 36in) square

cotton, sewing, matching fabrics

scissors

needle

OPTIONAL:

sewing machine

METHOD

1. From green material, cut a 90cm (36in) square for lining.
2. From full-size pattern cut 64 green triangles.
3. Make 4 green strips 7.5cm (3in) wide and 90cm (36in) long from remaining green material.

4. From full-size pattern cut 48 white triangles.
5. From full-size pattern cut 16 blue triangles.
6. Make 8 blue strips 3.75cm (1 1/2in) wide and 90cm (36in) long from remaining blue material.
7. Make 4 of the 'Peace and Plenty' blocks from the pieces of fabric. (See diagram.)
8. Join the 4 blocks together.
9. Add the blue strips of fabric around the four-block piece (log-cabin style.) (See diagram A.)
10. Add the green strips of fabric around the 4-block piece out-side the blue strip (log-cabin style). (See diagram B.)

TEMPLATE

The Contributor
The Irish Countrywomen's Association has over 25,000 members all over Ireland. There are no barriers of race, creed, class or political persuasion.
The Maker
Bernadette Falvey lives in Galway with her family, and says that she 'fell in love with patchwork' in 1981. It is now her abiding passion and hobby, and she tries to devote some time to it each day. She has been an active member of the Irish Countrywomen's Association for many years. Her work has been exhibited widely in Ireland and the UK, and in Austria. Her ambition is to explore all types of fabric art.

TEMPLATE Traditional 'Peace and Plenty' block

Scale 0.5cm – 7.5cm (1/4 – 3 in) approx.

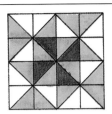

Make 4 of the above block as directed below

Row 1 + + +  =

Row 2 + + + =

Row 3 + + +

Row 4

A 1st strip →

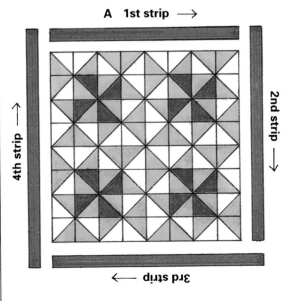

4th strip →

2nd strip →

← 3rd strip

B 1st strip →

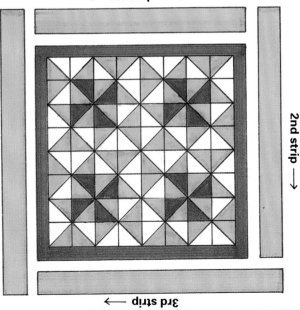

4th strip →

2nd strip →

← 3rd strip

93

11. Make a sandwich of: lining (wrong side up), batting on top of lining, patchwork on top of batting (right side up).

12. Pin or tack three layers together.

13. Machine or hand quilt, if desired.

14. Bind wall hanging with remaining blue strips.

15. Add sleeve at back, if desired, for hanging. (See below.)

To make sleeve:

1. Cut a piece of fabric 20cm (8in) wide, and as long as the width of the wall hanging.

2. Fold in half lengthways; sew up one end and the long side.

3. Turn inside-out, then turn in the other end and slip-stitch closed.

4. Pin this casing to the top of the wall-hanging, about 3cm (1¼ in) from the top; slip stitch top and bottom of casing to the backing of the wall-hanging.

✳ *HINT The block can be used on its own to make a cushion cover.*

The Silken Wall Hanging may take from 10 to 40 hours, close to the latter if you hand quilt. Cost will depend entirely on the fabric you choose. This is a gift that will hold your eye with its beauty.

CHILD'S COCKEREL SWEATER

by Vanessa Keegan

A flight of fantasy from Bolivia, this sweater was inspired by Paracas and Nazca pre-Columbian textiles of South America. It is fairly simple to make once you have mastered the technique, using small separate strands of yarn for each bird. It is also a good way to use up odd bits of coloured yarn.

This sweater is made in Alpaca, a soft luxurious yarn from an animal which looks a bit like a small camel without the humps! It can, of course, be made in any yarn of comparable thickness.

Step-by-step instructions

MATERIALS:

5 (6-6) balls of Jaeger Alpaca (or other 4-ply) yarn in main colour, Cream (MC)

1 ball (or small amounts) each in 9 colours: Royal (A); Aqua (B); Petrol (C); Olive (D); Turquoise (E); Bottle (F); Maroon (G); Purple (H); Yellow (I).

1 pair each of 2 ¼ mm (No.13) and 3mm (No.11) knitting needles.

6 stitch-holders or spare needles.

● *NOTES*
1. Letters refer to colours on chart.
2. Quantities of yarn given are based on average requirements and are therefore approximate.

MEASUREMENTS:

● *NOTE Figures in brackets refer to the larger sizes. Where only one figure is given, this refers to all sizes.*

To fit chest:
61 (66, 71) cm   24 (26, 28) in
Actual measurement:
71 (76, 81) cm   28 (30, 32) in
Length:
43 (48, 53) cm   17 (19, 21) in
Sleeve length:
33 (37, 41) cm   13 (14 ½, 16) in

TENSION:

28sts and 36 rows to 10cm (⅜ in) on 3mm (No.11) knitting needles over st.st.

ABBREVIATIONS:

k	knit
p	purl
st(s)	stitch(es)
st.st	stocking stitch
beg	beginning
foll	following
inc	increase

Opposite: *Child's Cockerel Sweater, Silken Wall Hanging*

dec   decrease
cont   continue
RS   right side
WS   wrong side
rep   repeat
rem   remaining
cm(s)   centimetre(s)
in(s)   inch(es)
tog   together

METHOD

Back

With 2 1/4mm (No.13) needles and MC, cast on 100 (108, 116) sts and work in *K2,P2* rib for 4cms (1 1/2ins).
Change to 3mm (No.11) needles** and work straight in st.st for 17 (20, 23) cms, 6 1/2 (7 3/4, 9)ins. Place chart.

K32 (36,40), now work 36sts from chart A, using separate balls of yarn for each colour block, winding yarns around each other at colour changes on every row to stop a hole forming, K32 (36,40).
Cont straight as set until 28th row of chart has been worked, thus ending with a WS row. Cont straight in st.st until back measures 43 (48,53)cms, 17 (18 3/4, 20 3/4)ins ending with a WS row. Leave sts on 3 holders in groups of 28 (32,36)sts; 44sts; 28 (32,36)sts.

Front

Work as for BACK to ** then work in st.st for 2 (12,22) rows. Place chart.

K2 (6,10), now work 96sts from chart B, using separate balls of yarn for each colour block, winding yarns around each other at colour changes on every row to stop a hole forming, K2 (6,10).
Cont straight as set until 112th row of chart has been worked, thus ending with a WS row. Cont straight in st.st until front measures 37(42,47)cms, 14 1/2 (16 1/2, 18 1/2)ins ending with a WS row.

Shape neck

Next row: K42 (46,50), leave rem sts on holder, turn and *** dec 1st at neck edge on every row until there are 28 (32,36)sts, ending with a WS row.

CHART A   Background colour and eyes are all in main colour   **CHART C**

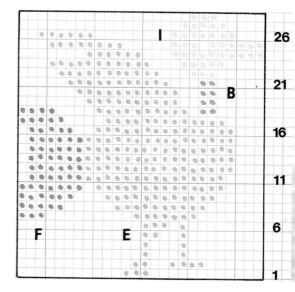

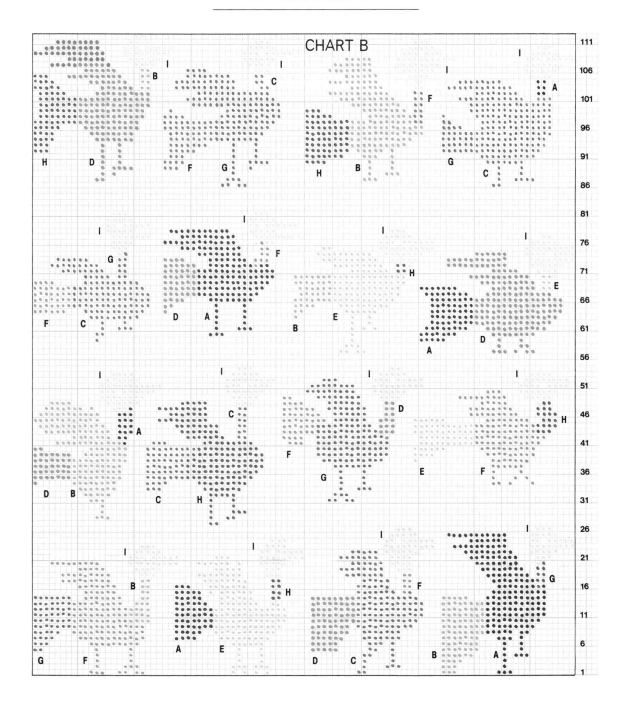

CHART B

Work straight for 6 rows, leave sts on holder.

Rejoin yarn to rem sts and K to end of row. Leave centre 16 stitches on holder. Now work from *** to end.

Sleeve

With 2 1/4 mm (No.13) needles and MC, cast on 30 (32,34)sts and work in K2,P2, for 4cms (1 1/2 ins). Change to 3mm (No.11) needles.
Increase row: K3 (2,1), inc in next st. *K1, inc in next st, rep from * to last 4 (3,2)sts. K to end. (42[46,50]sts)
Next row: P.
Place chart.
Inc in 1st st, K7 (9,11), work 26sts from chart C, K7 (9,11), inc in last st.
Cont in st.st working 28 rows of chart but at the same time inc 1 st at each end of 3rd and foll 4th rows until there are 92 (104, 116)sts, then work straight until sleeve measures 33 (37,41)cms. Cast off loosely.

Neckband

With 2 1/4 mm (No.13) needles and MC, with RS facing, pick up and K24sts down left front neck, K16sts from front holder, K24sts from right front neck and finally K44sts from back holder (108sts).
Work in *K1,P1* rib for 6cms (2 1/2 ins). Cast off ribwise loosely.

To finish:

With RS of shoulders together, K1st from front and 1st from back together loosely, rep with next 2sts then pass the first st over the second to cast off.
Rep to end of shoulder and fasten off. Work other shoulder in same way.
Press according to ball band instructions.
Measure and mark 18 (20,22)cms, 7 (7 3/4, 8 1/2)ins each side of shoulder then sew sleeves between these marks.
Join side and sleeve seams.
Turn neckband to inside and slipstitch neatly but loosely.

The Child's Cockerel Sweater will require some time and the cost of the wool. The result will be lasting and attactive.

The Maker
As a textile designer, I have been working for the last two years on a project funded by Oxfam Trading to work with Andean knitting groups to help improve their design and marketing. I live in Bolivia, working with three groups there, and one organisation in Peru which works with nearly 2,000 women in Juliaca near Lake Titicaca. By organising themselves into knitting production centres the women also have access to education and health programmes.

This child's sweater was made by La Imilla, an association of women in Arani, a small village about 60km (37 1/2 miles) outside of Cochabamba, Bolivia. They supplement their agricultural subsistence by knitting, offering an alternative to migration to conurbations or to Chapare, a major coca-growing area in Bolivia.

These four organisations are now selling some of their sweaters to well-known stores in Britain and the United States.

CHILD'S RAG BOOK

by Catherine Beadle for Wrencraft

This gift recalls the charm of rag books from the earlier years of this century. New machine-driven technology is contrasted in this child's rag book with traditional methods of farming, where work is done by hand with simple tools. The images of traditional methods are taken from pictures featured in many Oxfam leaflets and posters. Catherine Beadle lives in the heart of rural Holderness, Yorkshire, one of the most fertile agricultural regions in the country. For the title of this book, she has chosen the Oxfam Anniversary theme, 'It's Time for a Fairer World'. That means fairer for everyone, including farmers in Britain, where the little farms are disappearing, swallowed up by the 'giants'.

The rag book, made of folded strips of canvas, features 'Time' – a clock in simple cross-stitch on the front. This is useful for teaching children how to tell the time. The pages of the book show tractors, which children love. You can design your own pages to make a six-page book, using the 'Fairer World' theme. The book is environmentally friendly, indestructible and is made of cotton, so can be laundered and pressed easily.

● *NOTE Oxfam works with farmers throughout the Third World, collecting and sharing advice about the types of farming techniques that are best suited to their land and facilities. If you would like to know more about food and farming in the Third World, write to the Oxfam Information Department at 274 Banbury Road, Oxford, OX2 7DZ.*

Step-by-step instructions

MATERIALS:
Binca canvas, 6 blocks to 2.5cm (1in), 51cm (20in) wide, 76.5cm (30in) long
embroidery silks, assorted colours
cotton thread, matching
bias binding, 2.5cm (1in) wide, 30cm (12in) long, cherry red
needle, tapestry (No. 22)
scissors

Anchor stranded cotton:
black 403; dark grey 400; silver grey 397; red 47; bright yellow 297; gold 306; green 266; dark brown 360; orange 324 ; fawn 390; dark blue 137; white.

METHOD
Patterns are included for the front and back covers and two inner pages. If you would like to add two more pages, design your own pictures, reflecting the 'Fairer World' theme as you see it, OR agriculture in your part of the country OR (if you live on a farm) scenes from your farm.

1. Divide Binca canvas into 3 equal strips (for 6 page book), 51cm (20in) wide and 25.5cm (10in) deep.

✳ *HINT To prevent fraying, over-sew edges OR cover in masking tape.*

2. Fold each strip in half and mark centre line with a row of tacking stitches. Then mark out page area. Each page should be 55 squares wide, 46 deep (diagram 1).

● *NOTES*
1. If a design runs over two pages, it is essential that the design be POSITIONED ACCURATELY on the page, or the designs will not join up correctly when your book is made up.
2. The design is worked in cross-stitch and backstitch.
3. Six strands of thread are used, except for finer details (eg. outlining ears of wheat on cover; outlining the frame of the tractor; details on boy's face and bundle of hay and so on.)
4. Use a piece of thread approximately one metre (one yard) long to work.
5. Always work crosses so that the top stitches all lie in the same direction.

How to make up the book
1. Carefully trim off loose ends.
2. Press gently on wrong side.
3. With the right sides of the work facing each other, join together edges of pages by using 2 strands of sewing thread to work through the holes of the canvas along the tacked page line. (See diagram.)

4. Press seams open. The work should now form a continuous strip with the designs joined up. (See diagram.)
5. Fold each page along centre tacking line, and turn in the excess fabric at the top and bottom. Oversew the top and bottom edges to form the book pages.

6. Trim excess fabric in the 'spine' of the book to approximately 1cm (³/₈ in).
7. Oversew bias binding into place to neaten.

● *NOTE Catch the bias binding onto the top layer of fabric only in each case so book will open properly.*

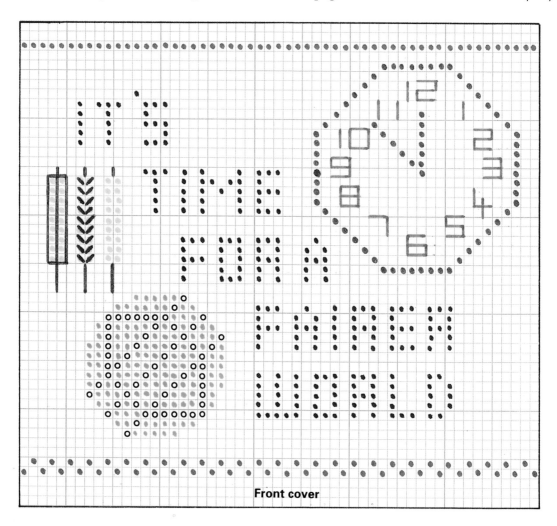

Front cover

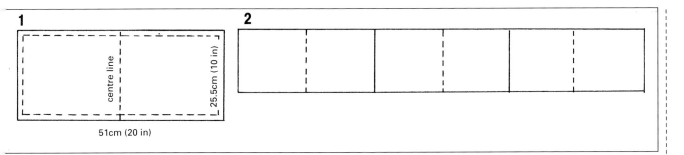

1

centre line

25.5cm (10 in)

51cm (20 in)

2

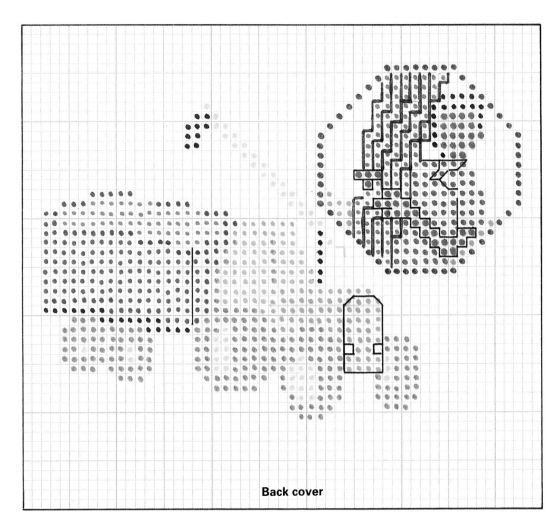

Back cover

The Maker

As a young child I spent hours copying my mother's Fair Isle knitting patterns into squared exercise books. At the age of ten I found a chart for a cross-stitch design in a magazine. It required even-weave linen. We didn't have any, so I drew squares on a piece of old sheet and used that instead. My fate was sealed, and then embroidery silks went up from tuppence to thrupence, and I wondered how my pocket money would stand it. I didn't know then that one day I would have a room filled with hundreds of miles of embroidery thread.

By the time I qualified as a Veterinary Surgeon my hobby was out of control. Then, I bought a needlecraft firm. Now, for designing, it's back to the squared exercise book again.

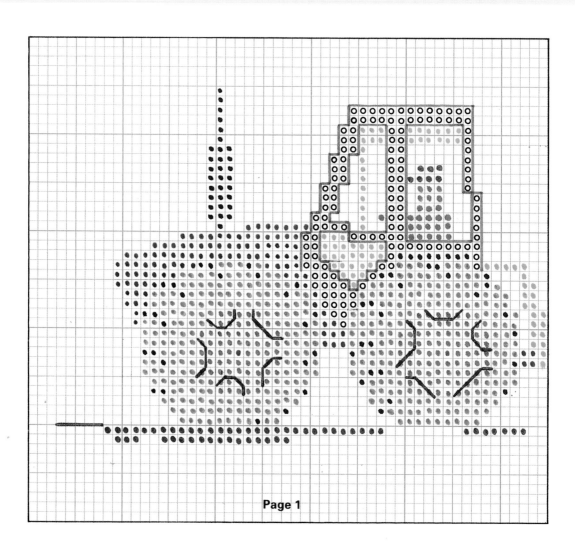

Page 1

8. Finally, neaten the top and bottom of the spine by oversewing the ends of the bias binding.

● *NOTE To wash: Gently hand wash. The book goes very 'floppy' when wet. Stretch back into shape. Dry flat.*

The Child's Rag Book is a unique gift, and easy to personalise. It could become a family treasure. The materials cost a little more than most gifts in this book, and it takes 24 to 36 hours to make. Either making it, or looking at it with children, this is a book no one will be able to put down.

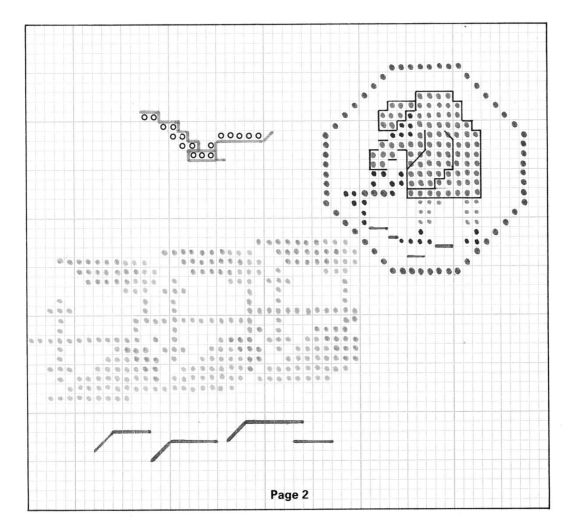

Page 2

OXFAM JUMPERS AND BLANKETS

For many years dedicated knitters have been making jumpers and blankets for Oxfam to send to people in need around the world. The knitting patterns and instructions are reproduced here for anyone who would like to make a gift for friends or family, or for Oxfam. Knitters can add their own embellishments and variations.

Step-by-step instructions

ABBREVIATIONS:

gst	garter stitch (every row knit)
K	knit
tog	together
st(s)	stitch(es)
dec	decrease
rept	repeat
in(s)	inch(es)
SLIK	slip stitch knitways
cm(s)	centimetre(s)
mm(s)	millimetre(s)

BABY COAT

This 4-ply baby coat will fit 45.5 and 50 cm (18 and 20in). It is easy to make and hard-wearing.

● *NOTE Requirements for 50cm (20in) are in brackets throughout.*

MATERIALS:
*3 (4) balls of wool, 20gm (^{3}/4 oz), of any 4-ply knitting wool
1 pair knitting needles, 3mm (No.11)
1 pair knitting needles, 2^1/4 mm (No.13)
1 stitch-holder*

METHOD
Using 3mm (No.11) needles cast on 159 (171) sts and work 66 rows in gst.
(Every row knit.)

Shape armholes:
K 41 (44) cast off 2 (2) K 73 (79) including sts on needle, cast off 2 (2) knit to end.

Left front:
Continue on first 41 (44) sts. Slip remaining sts on to a stitch-holder.
Continue in gst K 2 tog at armhole edge on next and every following 3rd row until 25 (28) sts remain, finishing at neck edge.
Cast off 8 sts at beg of next row, knit to end. Continue dec as before on every 3rd row. At the same time K 2 tog at neck edge on every row until 3 sts remain.
Next row. K 2 tog K 1.
Next row. K 2 tog. Fasten off.

Back:
Slip 73 (79) sts from stitch-holder on to a 3mm (No.11) needle. Rejoin wool and work in gst. K 2 tog at each end of the needle on the 4th and every following 3rd row until 35 (39) sts remain.
Work 1 row. Fasten off.

Right front:
Slip remaining 41 (44) stitches from stitch-holder on to a 3mm (No.11) needle and continue in gst as for left front, reversing all shapings.

Sleeves (both alike):
Using 2^1/4mm (No.13) needles, cast on 46 (50) sts.
Work 2.5cms (1in) K 1, P 1 rib.
Change to 3mm (No.11) needles
Work in gst until work measures 14cm (5^1/2 in) from commencement.

Shape top:
Cast off 2 (2) sts at beg of next 2 rows
K 2 tog at each end of the needle on the next and every following 4th row until 22 (22) sts remain.

Opposite: Boy wearing Oxfam Jumper at a Cheshire Home in Ethiopia.

K 2 tog each end of needle on the next and following alternate rows until 2 sts remain.
Cast off.

Making up:
Join sleeve seam by back stitching. With right side of work facing and using 2¼mm (No.13) needles pick up and knit 83 (87) sts evenly around neck edge.
1st row. K 1 * P 1 K 1 rept from * to end.
2nd row. P 1 * K 1 P 1 rept from * to end.
Rept 1st and 2nd rows once more. Cast off in rib. Press all seams flat.

If you are knitting for Oxfam:
The tops Oxfam receives are usually for babies and very young children.

They are in GREAT NEED of LARGER TOPS for the older child, and with a good-sized neck opening for comfortable wear. Oxfam would be very happy to receive tops at the upper end of the size range - around 81cm (32in) chest, so they may help a greater range of children in many parts of the world.

CHILDREN'S TOP

In 1991 alone, devoted Oxfam knitters created 286,800 tops, which Oxfam was able to send to a wide range of countries - from Ethiopia, Sudan and Angola to Iran and Iraq.

The quality of the knitting is almost invariably excellent and it is clear that much thought and hard work has gone into each garment's creation. This pattern is perfect for Oxfam.

● *NOTE Figures in brackets refer to the larger sizes throughout.*

MEASUREMENTS:
To fit chest:
51 (56, 61, 66, 71, 76, 81) cms
20 (22, 24, 26, 28, 30, 32) ins
Length from top of shoulders:
30 (34, 38, 42, 46, 49, 53) cms
12 (13½, 15, 16½, 18, 19½, 21) ins
Sleeve seam:
10 (13, 15, 17, 18, 19, 20) cms
4 (5, 6, 6½, 7, 7½, 8) ins

MATERIALS:
25g (1oz) balls of any Double Knitting wool: 6 (8, 9, 11, 12, 14, 15) balls
pair knitting needles: 3¼mm (No.10)
pair knitting needles: 4mm (No.8)

METHOD
Back and front (alike) with 3¼mm (No.10) needles cast on 56 (60, 66, 70, 76, 80, 86) sts and work 10 rows in garter stitch.
Change to 4mm (No.8) needles and continue in stocking stitch (one row knit and one row purl) until work measures 18 (20.5, 24, 26.5, 30, 32.5, 36) cms OR 7 (8, 9½, 10½, 12, 13, 14½) ins, ending with right side facing for next row.
Cast on 20 (26, 30, 32, 36, 38, 40) sts at beginning of the next two rows for sleeves 96 (112, 126, 134, 148, 156, 166) sts.
Next row SLIK, K to end. Repeat last row until work measures 30 (34, 37.5, 41.5, 45, 49) cms OR 12 (13½, 15, 16½, 18, 19½) ins.
Cast off.

To make up:
Join shoulder and upper sleeve seams leaving 18 (19, 19, 20.5, 20.5, 21.5, 21.5) cms OR 7 (7½, 7½, 8, 8, 8½, 8½) ins open at centre for the neck.

KNITTED BLANKETS

Currently Oxfam receives many blankets from dedicated knitters - 33,580 in 1991. They are shipped overseas to Oxfam-supported refugee centres, hospitals and orphanages.

Knitting a blanket is relaxing, giving a great feeling of achievement when you complete your colourful creation, and an even better feeling of satisfaction when you give it away.

What might your blanket be used for? Bedding and clothing, giving shade or carrying goods and children.

An easy way to make a standard blanket 1.8 x 1.2m (6 x 4ft):

1. Knit 12 strips, each measuring 1.2m (4ft) in length and 15cm (6in) in width, changing the colour of the wool every 15cm (6in).
2. Sew the strips together. This is quickly and easily done.

✱ *HINT The use of different colours helps you to keep the tension even when sewing up.*

This produces an evenly shaped, strongly stitched blanket, useful for you to give as a gift and useful to Oxfam to ship overseas to those in need.

MATERIALS AND NO. OF STITCHES:

Coloured squares: 15 cms (6-ins)

Wool	Needle size		No. of stitches
3 ply	3mm (3 $^3/_4$ mm), No.11 (9)		48 (42)
4 ply	3mm (3 $^3/_4$ mm), No.11 (9)		44 (39)
D/knit	4 $^3/_4$ mm, 3 $^1/_4$ mm, 4mm, 5mm	32, 37, 33, 30	
	Nos. 7, 10, 8, 6		

Blanket strips: 1.2 metres by 15 cms (4ft by 6ins)

3 ply	3mm (3 $^3/_4$ mm), No.11 (9)		48 (42)
4 ply	3mm (3 $^3/_4$ mm), No. 11 (9)		44 (39)
D/knit	4 $^3/_4$ mm, 3 $^1/_4$ mm, 4mm, 5mm	32, 37, 33, 30	
	Nos. 7, 10, 8, 6		

If you are knitting for Oxfam:

Blankets: All blankets donated to Oxfam should be a STANDARD SIZE – 1.8 x 1.2m (6 x 4ft).

Why?

a) This way, Oxfam can make maximum use of the knitters' much appreciated work. With a standard specification the blankets can be shipped in standard-size bales - simpler and cheaper.
b) And, the recipient acquires a more robust and versatile item.

(All blankets of a smaller size are sold through Oxfam's shops - earning money to help those most in need.)

Knitted squares: Oxfam strongly urges that all loose knitted squares be sewn up at a local level before they are donated to Oxfam.

Why?

They have received so many loose squares that they are unable to get them sewn up. So, take your good and hard work one step further and present Oxfam with a whole blanket.

A message from Oxfam: Happy knitting!

ABOUT OXFAM

The Oxfam Make-a-Gift Book brings together easy to make gifts from the kitchen, from the garden, to make and to sew. They have been contributed by supporters of Oxfam, both ordinary people and the famous, television and radio programmes, organisations and companies. Each gift in some way meets the Oxfam Anniversary Challenge, 'It's Time for a Fairer World,' in celebration of Oxfam's 50th Anniversary Year.

Every day millions of people in the countries of the South go without things we in the developed countries of the North take for granted: food, shelter, water, education, health care, and the right to make decisions about our own lives. For many poor people things are getting worse, not better.

Oxfam is helping people break out of their poverty by supporting them in efforts to make changes that will last.

The Early Years

In 1942 the world is at war. Most of Europe is occupied by Nazi forces, and innocent civilians are suffering. In Oxford, on 5 October 1942, a group of people form the Oxford Committee for Famine Relief. Its aim: to relieve the suffering of civilians in Greece, and to press for supplies to be allowed through the Allied blockade.

The Oxford Committee joins with Famine Relief Committees around the country to lobby British and Allied governments. A trickle of food is allowed into Greece before the war ends, but it is only after liberation in 1944 and the end of the blockade that the trickle becomes a more adequate supply.

The Oxford Committee raises funds and supplies for the Greek Red Cross to support the victims of conflict. Donations come in from appeals to the public, and through a temporary 'gift shop' (the forerunner of the later familiar Oxfam shop).

When peace comes in 1945 the Oxford Committee finds there is still work to do. More than 30 million refugees are moving across the borders of Europe - with no possessions, no homes and no future. The Oxford Committee (it doesn't change its name for another twenty years) raises money and collects clothing. The money pays for food and shelter, and the clothing is shipped to frightened and shattered families across Europe, even including Germany.

In June 1948 the first permanent Oxfam shop (a Gift Shop and Collecting Centre) opens in Broad Street, Oxford. There is still an Oxfam shop on the site.

The Oxford Committee doesn't disband. It continues to organise relief for refugees from conflict and for victims of natural disasters. In 1965 the charity adopts its telegram name, Oxfam, as its registered name. It expands its activities and its vision and continues on the road to becoming the Oxfam we know today.

Changing Times: Oxfam Overseas

Oxfam now works in seventy-seven countries and supports nearly 3,000 long-term development projects. Much of its work is in places where conflict makes life almost unsupportable for innocent victims. A common theme through Oxfam's development is the commitment to humanitarian help for people, irrespective of religious or political boundaries.

Oxfam still carries out much emergency work but is also committed to the wider and more lasting relief of suffering. It works alongside the very poorest people, supporting them in their efforts to break free of sickness, illiteracy, powerlessness and poverty. Through this work, it helps to challenge the exploitation and injustice that keeps people poor.

Oxfam staff keep in regular contact with project partners, giving support and advice and ensuring that grants are well spent.

Many self-help projects are small scale, needing minimal financial support. About a third of Oxfam grants are for under £3,000, but the impact of these small sums is considerable. After decades of experience, Oxfam knows that the projects most likely to succeed are those in which people are working for their own development.

On the following pages you will find very brief information on just a few of the thousands of projects that Oxfam has supported.

If you want to find out more about Oxfam in any particular country, contact your local Oxfam office.

Changing Times: Oxfam in the UK and Ireland

Since 1942 campaigning and education have been an integral part of Oxfam's work, informing people and governments in the rich world about ways of working with poorer people in the countries of the South as they

Above: Oxfam blankets, Dafur, Sudan.

tackle poverty and global injustice.

Oxfam also means 'Oxfam shops'. There are over 850 in the United Kingdom and Ireland, and shops in Germany, Italy and Gibraltar.

Many of the craft items in the Oxfam catalogue and shops come from groups supported by Oxfam's Bridge programme which provides a outlet for goods produced in self-help development projects, backed up by marketing and by training support.

Oxfam pioneered many charity fund-raising methods that are now commonplace. Over sixty per cent of Oxfam's funds in the UK and Ireland come from people making donations or a covenanted gift, buying Bridge goods, sending Oxfam Christmas cards, using Oxfam shops, leaving a legacy, or taking part in fund-raising events. Eighty per cent of this money is spent on overseas work and related campaigning and education.

Oxfam has spread across the world. What started in Oxford is now an international family linked to development organisations around the world.

Oxfam: Working for a Fairer World

Since 1942 Oxfam has given support irrespective of race, colour, gender, politics or religion. This support can come in many ways:

✳ an improvement in life for the woman who can draw water from a new well without having to walk many kilometres.

✳ shelter and support for a refugee, even for a short time.

✳ two meals a day, instead of one, as a result of improved agricultural methods.

✳ a landless farmer getting title to land, and with it the freedom to feed his family.

✳ relief given by someone who is prepared to listen to your troubles.

✳ the joy of a mother whose child's life has been saved by oral rehydration.

✳ the lifting of some oppression through the activity of an unknown friend in a far country, who cared enough to write to their MP.

Oxfam gives an opportunity for everyone to make this support possible, to make our world a fairer place. By buying this book you have already contributed, through the royalty Oxfam will receive.

Oxfam Blanket

110

There are other ways you can work with Oxfam for a fairer world. You could:
✳ give good quality books, toys, clothes or other things you no longer need to an Oxfam shop.
✳ save stamps or coins and drop them off at an Oxfam shop.
✳ organise a social event to raise money for Oxfam.
✳ talk to other people about ways of working for a fairer world and get yourself and them involved.
✳ volunteer your time and your skills to work with Oxfam - in a shop, as a campaigner, as a speaker, as a house-to-house collector, as a fund-raiser.
✳ introduce Oxfam to organisations to which you belong – to church groups, social clubs, playgroups, trades unions, professional bodies, sports clubs.

We hope that you enjoy making the gifts in this book, and that we can count on your support in the future.

OXFAM PROJECTS

Here are just a few of the thousands of projects that Oxfam has supported:

✳ BRAZIL Many projects support the Indian peoples of the Amazon basin
✳ INDONESIA Yasayan Dian Pertiwi Indonesia: a shredding machine for garbage collectors to recycle plastic.
✳ ZAIRE Fraternité Chrétienne de Malades et Handicapés: equipment and materials for a group of young people with disabilities to manufacture stationery goods.
✳ BOLIVIA Centro de Promoción de la Mujer: salaries, materials, transport and childcare costs for women's production project.
✳ COLOMBIA Comité Co-ordinador de Organizaciónes Campesinas: agricultural help for the cultivation of garden plots by rural women displaced by violence in Cordoba.
✳ INDIA Jagarana: support for rural development, vocational training and adult education in tribal communities.
✳ SUDAN Dar el Rahman Society: charcoal, wood and materials for disadvantaged families to start income-generating activities.
✳ PAKISTAN Presentation Convent Sargodha: support for screen-printing workshop for women.
✳ JAMAICA Groundwork Theatre Company: a grant for popular education work and street theatre.

To find out more about Oxfam contact us in:

ENGLAND
Oxfam Anniversary Information,
274 Banbury Road,
Oxford OX2 7DZ.

IRELAND
Oxfam,
202 Lower Rathmines Road,
Dublin 6.

NORTHERN IRELAND
Oxfam,
P.O. Box 70,
52-54 Dublin Road,
Belfast BT2 7HN.

SCOTLAND
Oxfam,
5th floor,
Fleming House,
134 Renfrew Street,
Glasgow G3 6ST

WALES
Oxfam,
46-48 Station Road,
Llanishen,
Cardiff CF4 5LU.

Organisations and Companies

As well as individual supporters of Oxfam, the following are among the organisations and companies that have helped with this book:

British Origami Society (BOS),
Penny Groom,
Membership Secretary,
2a The Chestnuts,
Countesthorpe,
Leicester LE8 3TL.

Designers of Distinction,
(Jessica and Jenny Bryne-Daniel),
Pant Gwyn,
Dyffryn Ardudwy,
Gwynedd,
Wales LL44 2HX.

Egg Crafters' Guild of Great Britain,
(Joan Cutts)
The Studio, 7 Hylton Terrace,
Coach Lane,
N Shields,
Tyne & Wear NE29 0EE.

Federation of Women's Institutes of Northern Ireland (FWINI),
209-211 Upper Lisburn Road,
Belfast,
Northern Ireland BT10 0LL.

The Henry Doubleday Research Association (HDRA),
National Centre for Organic Gardening,
Ryton-on-Dunsmore,
Coventry CV8 3LG.

The Herb Society,
P.O. Box 599,
London SW11 4RW.

Inverdene Vegan Guest House,
(Julie Campbell),
11 Bridge Square,
Ballater,
Aberdeenshire,
Scotland AB35 5QJ.

Irish Countrywomen's Association,
58 Merrion Road,
Dublin 4.

Knitting & Crochet Guild,
228 Chester Road North,
Kidderminster,
Worcestershire DY10 1TH

Knit-Knacks,
(Jane Platt),
16 Springfield Road,
Binfield,
Berkshire RG12 8TW.

National Association of Flower Arrangement Societies of Great Britain (NAFAS),
21 Denbigh Street,
London SW1V 2HF.

Patchwork & Quilting magazine,
(Elaine Hammond),
1 Highfield Close,
Malvern Link,
Worcestershire WR14 1SH.

Rag Rugs,
(Jenni Stuart-Anderson),
The Birches,
Middleton-on-the-Hill,
Leominster,
Herefordshire HR6 0HZ.

Rowan Yarns,
Green Lane Mill,
Holmfirth,
West Yorkshire HD7 1RW

The Royal Horticultural Society,
80 Vincent Square,
Victoria,
London SW1

Squirrel Services,
(Pam and Peter Redwood),
85 Silver Street,
Norwich, Norfolk NR3 4TU

Townswomen's Guilds,
Chamber of Commerce House,
75 Harborne Road,
Edgbaston,
Birmingham B15 3DA.

The Vegan Society,
7 Battle Road,
St Leonard's-on-Sea,
East Sussex TN37 7AA.

Wales Craft Council,
(Cyngor Craft Cymru),
Park Lane House,
7 High Street,
Welshpool,
Powys SY21 7SP

Wrencraft,
(Catherine Beadle),
The Manor House,
Skeffling,
Patrington,
Hull HU12 0UX.